Thierry PASTOR

In the shadow of Titans

Argos Collection

Thierry Pastor: graduate in law and political science, he has been working as a political advisor for about fifteen years. Initially trained in politics, he specialized in the geopolitics of energy and global security. He has worked in several regions of the world, mainly in Eastern Europe and Asia. He is the co-author of several books on the geopolitics of energy, written with university professors, lawyers and economic intelligence specialists. He works in collaboration with several experts with various skills: information systems, blockchain technology including cryptocurrencies, NFTs or metaverses. Thanks to this external expertise, these books were born.

TABLE OF CONTENTS

Foreword   p. 4
Towards a new world order?   p. 7
Election and undecided results   p. 50
Oil prices and the US presidential election   p. 77
Joe Biden and the American oil lobby   p. 102
Joe Biden's big challenge   p. 116
President Biden takes on China...and Donald Trump
                                                      p. 136
The first official meeting of Presidents Biden and Putin
                                                      p. 139
Effective US-European rapprochement in sight   p. 144
The thorny North Korean nuclear issue   p. 155
Israel-Palestine, the eternal re-start   p. 180
Victory of the ultraconservative Raissi in Iran   p. 194
Tensions, uncertainties and Covid   p. 197
New Covid-19 variant, new concerns   p. 203

Foreword

There is strength in numbers. It is from this premise that we decided to aggregate our skills and build our analyses. With different professional backgrounds and life experiences, we concluded that we had to work together because although we do not seem to come from similar worlds, we found many links. Nothing happens by chance. On the one hand, the scientists: engineers, programmers, precursors of the blockchain and fine connoisseurs of cryptocurrencies. On the other, the political advisor, specialist in political analysis, energy geopolitics and global security issues. Two apparently different worlds. And yet, one thing was obvious: our respective skills were complementary.

We noticed that what seems obvious or simple to understand is not so for most people. Few people can code, encrypt and develop computer programs. Few are also able to decipher the interconnections, the ins and outs that allow us to understand events for which most people will only have a limited understanding. Don't be fooled by this misplaced pretentiousness! In truth, we all have access to many things, but are we given the means to understand them? We assume that the answer is no.

Thanks to the Internet, everyone has access to a considerable flow of information. It is still necessary to be able to select, sort and discern those that provide the reader with a true understanding of things. One only must look at all the uncertainties surrounding the Covid-19 health crisis, the mass of information that contradicts itself and for which many grey areas remain. Our job is to try to understand what is going on around us: decipher, understand, and explain. Our objective, in all humility, is to try to shed light on political, economic, historical, technological, or other themes that will allow you to have another vision of the world around you.

Among the themes we will address, you will find blockchain, cryptocurrencies, energy issues, the evolution of international relations and power games, the emergence of green finance or ESG criteria. The list of topics covered is not exhaustive. However, EVERYTHING is linked! We try to highlight the bridges that link these elements that seem to be independent from each other. One should never trust appearances, especially in a world that is so globalized and even more connected due to technological progress.

Our methodology is as follows: all our publications are dated. Some factual or specific elements may seem obsolete. Certainly... but they have the merit of contextualizing the reflection that we develop. The objective is above all to identify trends, those that are likely to continue over time. The world of analysis is not an exact science, even more so when it deals with disciplines as variable and fluctuating as politics or international relations. We can therefore be wrong. On the other hand, we do our best to argue our points. But we can tell you this: the world is constantly changing... and everything is happening at a dizzying pace. Today's truth is not necessarily tomorrow's one. We must therefore live with the times and understand the causes of these changes. It is from this understanding that you will better understand current events and what surrounds you.

Our books compile reflections on different themes, some of which come up repeatedly. In such cases, it means that we give them a high importance. In our view, they are a major factor in the evolution of international relations, technologies and, more generally, in the major trends that are being set up. It is this last point that we are most interested in: we see that things are happening, but we do not fully understand the mechanisms. However, everything is done so that a new vocabulary is disseminated without it being explicitly defined or its inherent stakes being truly understood. This is what we are trying to do. Blockchain, cryptocurrencies, smart cities and other trendy concepts remain relatively nebulous. Yet they fit perfectly into a political, diplomatic, economic, and more globally societal evolution that we are experiencing at a very high speed. The puzzle is large. It is up to everyone to gather the pieces which compose it and to assemble them.

Towards a new world order?
September 2021

The tumultuous departure of Westerners from Afghanistan under the close watch of the Taliban, back in force in Kabul, is an image that will remain associated with new geopolitics of Central Asia that is being put in place. Although the Taliban have never really disappeared from the country since their departure from power in 2001, the much-feared scenario has finally occurred: after twenty long years in the country, the coalition forces are leaving under unexpected conditions. It was unexpected because no one expected the Taliban to arrive so quickly and easily at the gates of the capital. The immediate reaction of many Afghans rushing to the city's airport in the hope of leaving their homeland as soon as possible is striking. The hope of a definitive departure was the only prospect for them not to experience again an extremely strict political regime such as the one imposed by the Taliban between 1996 and 2001.

Beyond the human drama that seems to be becoming clearer and clearer every day with the new masters of the country, who do not seem to be implementing what they had promised when they returned to Kabul, the chaotic departure of foreigners and Afghans who collaborated with Western powers highlights a reality: the armed intervention was a resounding failure. In 2001, it drove out the Taliban and heralded a new era of social peace that never came. The Taliban took refuge in mountainous and sparsely populated areas. They managed to maintain control over some areas. Indeed, they never disappeared from the Afghan landscape.

As early as the 2000s, there were debates among the new national leaders, with some suggesting the option of negotiating with a more moderate fringe of the Taliban. This prospect was never taken up by the Western powers, for whom a Taliban association with Afghan power was unthinkable. Two decades after the first armed intervention, the departure of the Westerners does not only mark the end of an unfinished military mission. The strong image of the Taliban controlling all the access roads to the only Afghan exit is above all indicative of a debacle that looks like a slap in the face for the United States and NATO. The Taliban's refusal to grant permits beyond August 31, 2021, for the evacuation of foreigners and Afghans wishing to leave the country is the height of humiliation, which highlights the limits of armed intervention despite the resources mobilized. No one knows if the new Taliban era will be sustainable or not. It will, insofar as the armed opposition will be limited in terms of men and means that aim at reconquering the country. As for the Western powers, they will have done no better than the British Empire in the 19th century and the USSR in the 1980s: Afghanistan has remained an untamed land. The Western world suddenly saw its international credibility slip away.

The U.S. military's poor intelligence on the Taliban advance toward Kabul is the latest example of an international intervention that has never been able neither to control nor contain its adversaries. While many Western countries had already begun to evacuate their nationals, some also opted to close all forms of diplomatic representation in Afghanistan. A minority retained a diplomatic presence until the last days granted by the Taliban, but the latter already seemed to be establishing rules that were out of step with the promises made during press conferences, and many countries were reluctant to consider a future and new diplomatic presence in Kabul. However, when faced with the return of the Taliban, not everyone reacts in the same way. Russia indicated that it wanted to see what the new Taliban governance would look like. It decided to maintain diplomatic representation, suggesting that dialogue with the Taliban was an option. As for China, it not only maintains a diplomatic presence but also intends to continue to defend its economic interests. Sometime before the conquest of Kabul, the Chinese Foreign Minister received a delegation of senior Taliban officials in Beijing, a clear sign that China does not want to change its ambitions because of a change in political governance in Afghanistan.

More generally, the end of the Western presence in Afghanistan is marking a turning point in contemporary international relations. Above all, it marks a new failure in the fight against terrorism and authoritarian regimes. Iraq was the first example. Afghanistan has only confirmed the Iraqi scenario. In both cases, political destabilization occurred: the Taliban were pushed out in 2001; in Iraq, Saddam Hussein was captured, and his regime collapsed. The problem is that in both cases, the Western world sought to establish new democratic regimes, but they came up against another reality: terrorism.

Terrorism regularly and severely hit both the civilian population and the foreign armed forces in Iraq and Afghanistan. Despite the human, logistical and financial resources deployed in these two countries, terrorist organizations have constantly contributed to maintaining a climate of fear. And the ruling political elites have never succeeded in establishing a lasting social peace. It is not surprising, therefore, that Iraq experienced a surge in violence when Daesh proliferated in Syria following the Arab Spring and then ventured into parts of Iraq. As for the Taliban, although they are opposed to Daesh, they have been patiently preparing their return to business in Kabul. In other words, after two decades of foreign presence in both countries, the socio-political situation is not only out of control but even more chaotic.

In Afghanistan, the forced departure of the Taliban in 2001 has finally led to the departure of the West in 2021 and the return of the outcasts of yesteryear. As for Iraq, the end of Saddam Hussein's regime has brought desolation to a country that is unable to rebuild itself. The Western paradigm of fighting terrorism and authoritarian regimes has been severely tested. Whether in Iraq or Afghanistan, the conclusion is the same: the West has failed in its interventions. Not only are the targeted countries now at the mercy of terrorist organizations or those determined to oppose the Western world, but the global geopolitical reality tends to show above all that Western *hard* and *soft power* [1] is no longer as dominant as in the past. The hasty evacuation of Afghanistan symbolizes this failure. In short, civilian populations will certainly seek to flee war-torn lands. A new wave of migration will sweep across Europe in the coming months.

This dramatic reality for these people who want to find a better life in a peaceful environment will undoubtedly create new dissensions within the European Union (EU), which is already deeply divided on migration issues. Similarly, NATO member states are questioning the future of the Atlantic alliance, while the precipitous departure

---

[1] Author's note: *hard power* and *soft power* are theories of international relations. They originate from Joseph Nye, an eminent political scientist and author of numerous internationally recognized books and articles. He was Assistant Secretary of Defense for International Security Issues under President Clinton from 1994 to 1995. He defends the thesis that *hard power* is characterized by the traditional means of pressure within the political and military power relations. *Soft power* is based on a more subtle and flexible power of influence. It can be translated into economic or cultural policies. With Robert Keohane, he founded neoliberal institutionalism, a theoretical vision of international relations in which the power of institutions is great in the international system. Joseph Nye is one of the great names in international relations theory and one of the prestigious references of liberal thought.

from Afghanistan is pushing European states to demand explanations from the United States. In the front line, President Biden is targeted. The latter finds himself in a very uncomfortable position since his decisions concerning the general evacuation of Afghanistan are being contested. He gives the impression of being subjected to the situation. This does not fail to raise questions in the United States. The polls tend to show that his choices are misunderstood and disapproved by the Americans. As for the Republican opposition, it will not fail to denounce President Biden's management of the Afghan crisis in preparation for the mid-term elections that will take place in November 2022.

More generally, it is the entire Western world that is coming out groggy of the Afghan experience. As for the Sino-American rivalry, it is asserting itself a little more each day. Some analysts now fear that the next focus of crisis will be the island of Taiwan, a territory recognized as independent by most states in the world, but which China refuses to recognize as such, considering it to be Chinese territory. The recent military maneuvers carried out by China and the United States in the China Sea show above all that the two great rivals are seeking to intimidate each other. Anything goes. As for the return of the Taliban to Kabul, it plays more in Beijing's favor as it suddenly sees Western influence waning in Central Asia, a region where the Chinese capital is investing more and more in the deployment of its Silk Roads initiative.

Western domination in decline?
The question arises with the astonishing and tumultuous evacuation of foreign nationals from Afghanistan and Afghan citizens who fear for their lives because of the return of the Taliban to control the country. The end of the Western presence in Afghanistan ends with a bang. It symbolizes a major failure for the coalition forces

that have been there for two decades and have never succeeded in neutralizing the enemy forces, who are not only back in business... They are back, triumphant and convinced that they have dissuaded the West from risking a new military intervention, considering that the one that is ending is a failure. Thus, the Taliban are back after twenty years, and the Afghan people must prepare for a new period of governance dominated by extreme rigor. In other words, when the coalition intervention began in 2001, the goal was to hunt down the terrorists behind the 9/11 attacks. Afghanistan was immediately targeted because it was home to many members of the al-Qaeda organization that claimed responsibility for the attacks. The crimes could not go unpunished.

In the eyes of the United States, it was necessary to fight against this terrorist organization led by Osama bin Laden. Its allies were also fought. The Taliban were thus in the firing line and in a very short time they were forced to leave Kabul. This gave hope for better days for the Afghan population, but the hopes were short-lived. The Taliban, although weakened, never really left the Afghan life. The Taliban gradually gained influence in many areas where the coalition forces had great difficulty in controlling the territory. The military intervention quickly became engulfed in a difficult struggle. Even the capital city of Kabul was never a safe space, with the threat of terrorism looming at every turn. Despite the efforts of soldiers, logistics, and budgets devoted to rebuilding the Afghan state and other efforts to secure the country, nothing was done. Terrorist organizations continued to disrupt the momentum toward pacification in a country that had been at war for nearly three decades at the start of the new millennium.

In 2021, the Taliban returned to the forefront, confident of their strength. The conditions for the evacuation of foreign nationals and Afghans wishing to leave their country for security reasons put the Western world in a very uncomfortable position: the armed struggle has never negated the chances of a return of the Taliban or any other organization for that matter. Secondly, the process of nation-building is punctuated by an abject failure. The Western world is leaving the country in particularly chaotic conditions, with the Kabul airport symbolizing the only hopeful option for those seeking to leave, while the Taliban control all the communication routes to the country. On August 26, 2021, five days before the evacuation deadline, several explosions occurred near the airport, killing many people, including American soldiers. Shortly thereafter, the Taliban officially condemned the attacks. A few hours later, the attacks were claimed by Daesh, an organization fought by the Taliban. In the aftermath, President Biden declared that he would be intransigent against the culprits.

Still, the end of the American presence in Afghanistan is ending with an outcome that will undoubtedly have consequences for international relations in the coming years. It seems that American power has never been so challenged or put to the test since the end of the Cold War. In its wake, it is the entire Western alliance that will now have to ask itself about the consequences of a double failure in the fight against terrorism and in nation-building. There was indeed the period of decolonization that occurred during the Cold War which undoubtedly weakened the power of European states on the international scene, but these states were allies of the United States, which was then engaged in its opposition to the USSR and its communist allies. At the end of the Cold War, the United States became the world's most dominant power, and there was no reason to believe that this domination would be challenged twenty years later with the occurrence of the September 2001 attacks. However, the American leadership has been strongly shaken by the Afghan and Iraqi episodes, as well as by the Arab Springs that occurred at the beginning of the 2010s.

The landscape of international relations will be profoundly altered because of the Afghan crisis. The legitimacy and credibility of the Western world are being impacted and challenged. The August 26 attacks claimed by Daesh are above all the expression of a disorder or *fitna* that is even greater than it seems between states and the terrorist organizations they are fighting on the one hand; between terrorist organizations that are also fighting each other on the other. Daesh is striking in a country that the Taliban want to control, at a critical moment, since the evacuation of foreign nationals and Afghans is taking place in an extremely tense atmosphere in which the Taliban is not showing any leniency, merely retorting to the Western world that no additional time will be granted beyond August 31 to carry out the extractions desired by the West. President Biden's reaction, a mixture of empathy and anger, is naturally understandable, but one question remains: when he expresses his intention to track down the culprits of the August 26 explosions, what does he intend to put in place and where? While the military withdrawal from Afghanistan continues and it is undeniable that the joint intervention by the United States and its allies has had a negative result, can we imagine a new strong American or collegial mobilization and intervention of long duration to fight Daesh? The answer lies with Washington, but a response in the form of a war against Daesh must be approached in two ways.

First, initiate a new intervention to show the international community US hard power leadership. This strategy has its risks, including the risk of once again engaging in a grueling, costly struggle in terms of lives and money, which may lead to an uncertain outcome. Second, refusing to re-engage in a sustained conflict. This option would likely be criticized if no action is taken against those responsible for the Kabul attacks. The United States must be firm and unyielding. In sum, the most likely option remains a targeted and timely intervention. The major problem is that Daesh forces are spread over huge territories, and it will be difficult to locate the culprits over such a large area. The search for those behind the August 26 attacks will not be easy for the United States. However, President Biden must find them. His political credibility in the United States is at stake. The credibility of the United States on the international scene is also at stake. If Washington fails again, it will only confirm a trend: American dominance is increasingly challenged.

A new era is beginning

On several occasions in the history of the 20th century, thinkers have referred to a *new world order* following major changes in international relations. If it is difficult to define the new world order concept or theory. It is necessary to consider a major evolution leading to an impacting change in international relations. At the end of the First World War, one of the consequences was the disappearance of the great empires of the time: Prussia, Russia, Austria-Hungary, and the Ottoman Empire. This led to the creation of many new independent and sovereign states. Similarly, the outcome of the Second World War proposed a new world order with the lasting irruption of the Cold War and then, a decade later, the beginnings of decolonization, which definitively initiated the decline of European powers on the scene of international relations and the confrontation of the two dominant superpowers of the time: the United States and the USSR.

For four decades, the world functioned with an ideological opposition interspersed with critical periods and others of détente. When the Cold War ended with the collapse of the USSR, a new and unprecedented period began: for the first time in history, one country would establish an unparalleled dominance in terms of hard and soft power. A decade later, the events of September 11, 2001, were the trigger for a new form of opposition: the war on terrorism. It resulted in long and costly military interventions in Iraq and Afghanistan, while at the same time foreign powers emerged both economically and politically to the unexpected point of seriously challenging the overwhelming leadership of the United States.

The 2000s marked a major turning point in international relations. Wars against terrorism, the assertion of the rise of Russia and China, the gradual increase in challenges to US hegemonic dominance, the narrowing of the gap in economic, political, and military power between the US and China, etc., all contributed to the fact that US ultra-dominance was no longer so pronounced but was now being credibly opposed. Since the 2000s, it has become increasingly clear that international relations are evolving towards a world order driven by an enduring rivalry between the United States and China. China has patiently implemented public policies that have allowed it to ensure its irresistible rise to economic and political power, while its ambitions are no longer a mystery: it intends to become the world's leading economic power.

The beginning of the 21st century has also been marked by great maneuvers. The United States has never underestimated China's rise to power and has undertaken to make it more difficult for China to gain access to oil, a natural resource that is so important for the proper functioning of the Chinese economic model. China's demand for oil has continued to grow. Still self-sufficient in black gold until the mid-1990s, the period of sustained strong economic growth corresponded to an explosion in the demand for oil and forced China to become an importer. The need was such that in less than two decades it became the world's largest importer of crude oil. For the United States, it appeared that access to oil was a potential weakness for China: it was effectively dependent on the outside world to meet its domestic needs. However, not only has it always managed to meet its demand, but the second half of the 2000s was to be the confirmation that China's economic power could allow Beijing to find adequate solutions to ensure its energy needs. This is what China did in Central Asia, where the economic investments made gradually reduced Russia's influence in the former Soviet republics of the region.

In the 2010s, the arrival of Xi Jinping to power marked a new level of Chinese ambitions. The project to restore the Silk Roads is with no doubt without equal in history. It mobilizes considerable financial, logistical, and human resources. It also reflects China's desire to no longer confine itself to the role of an emerging power that would inevitably come up against American domination. China is moving forward and does not care much about American admonitions. Its power is becoming ever more assertive. Internal Chinese affairs that have generated waves of indignation in the West (Tibet, Xinjiang, or Hong Kong) have never pushed Beijing to back down. China openly displays its military power and has engaged in a strong-arm wrestling match with maneuvers in the China Sea or by reiterating its intentions concerning the island of Taiwan, a small state for which it has never recognized neither independence nor sovereignty. In Beijing's eyes, Taiwan is a part of China.

For a decade, the US-China opposition has been growing in intensity. The battle is being waged over new technologies, particularly digital (cyberattacks, 5G, etc.), but also in the field of armaments and even scientific laboratories... The end of American ultra-domination is over. If we are not talking about an American decline, it seems to us that it is the rise of China that has made American power no longer hegemonic. Indeed, a duel of titans has taken shape and seems set to animate international relations for several decades. The gap between the United States and China and the rest of the world in terms of hard and soft power is considerable. Russia is one of the major players in world politics and diplomacy, but its economic power is not comparable to that of the United States or China. The battle of the leaders is between the United States and China, and that American supremacy is no longer comparable to that of the post-Cold War era. The world has changed considerably since then.

The affirmation and exacerbation of Sino-American rivalry

The rise of the Chinese economy in the 2000s, however, left some analysts skeptical that it would be sustainable and, above all, able to compete with the US economy a few years later. The question was mainly about Beijing's ability to react the day economic growth rates started to slow down. China has indeed experienced a slowdown in economic growth but has managed to maintain dynamic rates. Its leaders benefited from an international environment that they took advantage of. The paradox is that everyone was aware of the exceptional performance of the Chinese economy, while Beijing kept a low profile. Gradually, it became clear that the United States would have to deal with a competitor that was beginning to take on various characteristics of an economic superpower. When Xi Jinping became China's leader, China's attitude changed dramatically: from being discreet, the capital of the Asian giant was now going to show its ambitions in broad daylight and, above all, confirm its desire to become the world's leading economic power.

The ambitious project of restoring the Silk Roads (the One Belt, One Road, OBOR initiative) has no equivalent in history. A country was willing to build large-scale communication routes to promote trade around the world. The Chinese economic model is indeed based on exports. Beijing intends to optimize its economic model by making the necessary investments to build or develop roads, railways, ports, and other facilities to facilitate the flow of economic exchanges. In the same way, all these new infrastructures financed by China must ensure the imports necessary for its good internal functioning. It is said that one thousand billion dollars have been earmarked for these immense works.

Skeptical analysts saw this project as overly ambitious and lacking in pragmatism, believing that it was either unfeasible or that it would impact China's economic health. China has never invested abroad at undue risk. It invests and hopes to get a return on its investment. It can convince countries to build new roads, railways, ports, and other facilities for which it provides the financing, but which always have a counterpart. When the partner cannot repay, China systematically finds a solution that allows it to limit its financial risks. By investing so much, it not only shows its economic strength but also progressively increases its political influence, although it never shows that it intends to concern itself with international politics as the United States or the EU may do.

China has patiently put in place its strategy to "conquer" the world, to extend its commercial web. It is aware of its need to export, as its domestic market is not sufficient for its economic model. In the 2000s, it embarked on a vast investment program in Central Asia, in the former Soviet republics, to secure massive supplies of hydrocarbons. Chinese money soon convinced the Central Asian leaders to negotiate with Beijing, while the traditionally influential foreign power in the region, Russia, lost its strategic influence. Indeed, the construction of new pipelines was to change the face of the hydrocarbon trade. The existing pipeline networks were all routed back to Russia, which allowed Moscow to maintain leverage over Kazakhstan, Turkmenistan, and Uzbekistan. The construction of new oil and gas routes that no longer cross Russia allowed China to increase its influence in Central Asia. When President Xi Jinping became the Chinese leader, the national ambitions were not only confirmed but also took on a new dimension with the OBOR project: China no longer wanted to make a secret of its real ambitions and sent an unequivocal message to the international community. Nothing should stand in the way of China becoming the world's economic leader.

The rise in economic power has not been achieved alone: China has also embarked on the development of high-level scientific and technological research programs. Like one of the great oppositions of the Cold War, China has embarked on the conquest of space. It has ambitious projects for the Moon or scientific missions on Mars. It has joined the closed circle of nations that have the economic means and scientific skills to finance space programs. On the other hand, the Huawei affair has highlighted another reality: China is among the most successful countries in terms of new technologies. China's evolution is even more striking given that in the 1990s, the country was at best an emerging power in the eyes of the Western world. In a quarter of a century, in many respects, it has become the global benchmark in certain fields of activity. China's modernization progress has been considerable. The same is true in the military sphere. In recent years, the country's defense budget has continued to grow. Beijing is acquiring high-quality weapons. The same is true for naval and air force equipment. This is what worries many analysts specialized in defense issues: what message is China sending? Does it intend to prepare for a military conflict?

President Xi Jinping gives the image of a self-confident and unyielding man who defends the interests of his country. He does not intend to give in to any American influence. As for Washington's demands, he brushes them aside with a wave of his hand. China is going its own way and is not concerned about external reactions. It has demonstrated this with Xinjiang and Hong Kong. Although international critics condemn the fate of the Uyghurs or the democracy of Hong Kong, Beijing does not waver. Beijing has decided and Beijing is doing. No one will be able to make it go backwards. On the international level, the same is true. The Chinese capital has never shown any reluctance to negotiate with the Taliban. That is why it is keeping a close eye on the nuclear activities developed by its neighbor North Korea. The case of North Korea's denuclearization is also highly indicative of China's new influence in world politics.

When President Trump ventured to announce his intention to bring the Pyongyang regime to heel by securing the country's total denuclearization through his sharp negotiating skills, he underestimated Beijing's leverage in Pyongyang. Although China has already voted for sanctions against North Korea in the United Nations Security Council, it has a vested interest in having an ally that continues to confound American ambitions in the Far East. While Donald Trump met twice with Kim Jong-Un on neutral ground (once in Singapore and the other time in

Hanoi), in the days leading up to these meetings, the North Korean leader went to Beijing, although he hardly ever leaves his country, to seek advice from Xi Jinping. One thing is clear: Donald Trump's diplomacy with North Korea is a failure. In other words, it is a Chinese victory. Although a military confrontation between the United States and China seems unlikely (although it is not non-existent), the American withdrawal from Afghanistan suggests an increase in American troops in the China Sea (which implies increased surveillance between the world's two leading economic powers). The reason is Taiwan. The former Formosa has never been recognized by Beijing as an independent and sovereign state. Taiwan could be the next confrontation between Beijing and Washington. The problem is that unlike the Cold War, when the United States and the USSR intervened in conflicts by interposition, the Taiwan question puts the United States and China in direct opposition.

A changing American strategic vision

The U.S. disengagement from Afghanistan confirms Washington's global vision of focusing its attention on China. Overseas troop deployment efforts will now be concentrated in areas geographically close to China. The withdrawal from Afghanistan should not obscure the reality that while the departure of the Americans had been planned for a long time, the outcome of the interventional mission is a failure. By evacuating its last troops, the United States is putting an end to a twenty-year war that will have ended in a rapidly predictable disappointment. This scenario was indeed conceivable since Afghanistan has never been pacified. Although elections were held after the departure of the Taliban in 2001, even the capital city of Kabul has never been safe, under constant threat from frequent and deadly terrorist attacks. Once again, the Taliban never completely disappeared from the Afghan landscape.

The same is true of the al-Qaeda organization, which has been able to move between Afghanistan and Pakistan. The operation that led to the fall of Osama bin Laden never resulted in the extinction of this network. Each loss of a leader is immediately compensated by the enthronement of a new one. Later, the Daesh began to express ambitions for Afghanistan, which contributed to further chaos, since the Taliban and Daesh do not like each other. Despite the deployment of nearly one hundred and fifty thousand foreign troops at a time when the international presence was strongest, the American command has never succeeded in reducing, let alone annihilating, the threats of socio-political destabilization in Afghanistan. To Washington's credit, this part of Central Asia is extremely difficult to control despite the use of high technology. Taliban forces have never outnumbered those of the international coalition, but this wilderness has remained as inaccessible as it once was to the British Empire or the USSR. No one has ever managed to "tame" Afghanistan. When the American intervention was originally decided, neither the White House nor the Pentagon imagined that the military presence would be so long.

However, it is important to remember the context at the time. The American presidential elections of 2000 were marred by doubts about the recount. For several months, the national political scene was in turmoil because the election of George W. Bush only gained real legitimacy with the occurrence of the attacks of September 11, 2001. For almost a year, the United States was divided between Republican and Democrat supporters who claimed victory for George W. Bush for the former and Al Gore for the latter. The debates and disputes were lively... and then came September 11. From that day on, all attention was focused on the need to identify, track down and capture the culprits. This is how Afghanistan became a target for intervention.

On the other hand, President Bush's inner circle was sympathetic to neo-conservative views. In the 2000s, while the war in Afghanistan was still going on and another front had meanwhile been opened in Iraq, the neo-cons had already identified China as a potential future threat to the United States. In sum, while the military intervention in Afghanistan had been fully justified by the attacks of September 11, 2001, the United States had deployed a strategy of presence in Central Asia that was really aimed at thwarting China's oil supplies. George W. Bush's advisers understood that there was a correlation between China's dynamic economic growth and its increasing oil needs. Thus, ways had to be found to prevent China from gaining easy access to oil. As it turned out, the American plans ran into many difficulties, especially in the former Soviet republics of Central Asia, where the loss of Russian influence was immediately seized upon by China, which managed to obtain satisfaction by negotiating the construction of new oil routes to the East. This situation satisfied the former Soviet republics, which were emancipating themselves from Russian influence, which was obvious because, once again, most of the hydrocarbon resources exported by Kazakhstan, Uzbekistan and Turkmenistan passed through pipeline networks that then went back to Russia. These new independent supply routes suddenly changed the geopolitical landscape in Central Asia. China gradually became a privileged economic partner.

The United States could not fight this economic reality, especially since Chinese investments were welcome in Almaty (Kazakhstan's major economic pole), Tashkent, or Ashgabat. In the meantime, China had also taken care to ensure strategic partnerships with Iraq, Iran, and Saudi Arabia. In a few years, Beijing managed to find the right solutions to ensure its growing hydrocarbon imports. In other words, the neo-conservative strategic vision was defeated by subtle Chinese diplomacy. It was doubly so since Chinese influence in Central Asia has never ceased to grow. On the other hand, the war in Afghanistan was dragging on desperately. When it was decided to withdraw US troops from Iraq and Afghanistan and not to get too involved in Syria, it was clear that, despite its fighting power, the US military had to face the facts and conclude that the fight against terrorism and the assistance provided in the nation-building process were insufficient. The Taliban were summoned from power in 2001.

They returned in force in 2021. As for Iraq, since the fall of Saddam Hussein, the country lives, like Afghanistan, in permanent socio-political chaos. This is what makes critics say that the United States intervenes, turns things upside down and leaves when it finds it has no control over the situation. The reality is much more complex. American investments and war efforts are real. They have certainly not succeeded in containing the terrorist threat or in establishing any kind of lasting socio-political peace. In many respects, the interventions in Afghanistan and Iraq were failures. The strategic dimension should not be overlooked: in this case, what is Washington most concerned about these days? It is obviously the growing rivalry with China.

Thus, the United States is focusing its attention on this rivalry, which is tending to intensify, and the "Western" arc of American presence in the greater Middle East is being abandoned in favor of the East, where Washington intends to expand its presence. The Eastern arc is now favored. Here again, this strategy is not new, since the United States has a significant presence in South Korea, Japan, and the Philippines until 2020, when Manila decided to break the bilateral military agreement. The issue that concerns Washington the most is Taipei, the capital of Taiwan. This island has been a matter of debate for several decades, since it is recognized as an independent and sovereign state by the entire Western world, while Beijing considers the island to be Chinese territory. While the Sino-American rivalry continues to grow, the strategic issue around the former Formosa is more sensitive than ever since Beijing and Washington are in direct opposition. It is not insignificant that the two countries have been conducting military maneuvers in the China Sea for several months and that they have a permanent presence there. The two countries are testing each other, and the fact that hard power is at the heart of this opposition may lead to fears of an escalation of tensions. It is certain that the idea that drives the two capitals is not to confront each other directly in an armed conflict whose consequences could be devastating on a large scale.

The United States and China have nuclear power as well as high-tech weapons with great destructive potential. In sum, the military threat is likely to remain a means of intimidation, while the real "war" between the two countries is fought on other grounds: new technologies, cyberattacks, customs barriers and even a war of scientific laboratories... Many areas can effectively highlight this rivalry, and there is no need to tip over into the extreme of an armed conflict to seal the domination of China or the United States. As a result of this observation, the interventional priorities of the U.S. military have changed and are now focused on the growing rivalry with China.

The confirmation of a clash of civilizations
In the 1990s, two major works were published that sought to understand what the world would become after the end of the Cold War. The first work published was by Francis Fukuyama in 1992. *The End of History and the Last*

Man [2] defends the thesis that liberalism and democracy have finally triumphed. However, this does not prevent the existence of conflicts, but the author postulates that liberal democracy will eventually prevail. In 1993, Samuel Huntington developed another thesis in an article published in Foreign Affairs [3], in which he attempted to describe the contemporary world through the prism of different civilizations that would not systematically manage to get along, but rather would end up displaying their differences, while power relations would always constitute an immutable component of international relations. Samuel Huntington's vision was based on a double paradigm: that of a multipolar and multi-civilization world.

In the 1990s, this thesis was widely criticized because the end of the Cold War left the international community in an unprecedented situation with the overwhelming domination of one nation in the world, whether it be hard or soft power. In this case, the end of the Cold War corresponded to the end of an ideological confrontation, but above all it saw the collapse of a system that had been based on communism and the thought of Lenin in particular. For this reason, Francis Fukuyama's vision was welcomed since the inevitable victory of liberal democracy over authoritarian communist systems was unquestionable. A new world order was shaped by this opposition, which lasted four decades. The American hyperpower was never so dominant. However, during this same decade, several factors appeared but were probably underestimated at the time. The USSR had disappeared from the international political landscape and new independent states were created. Russia had to rebuild itself.

---

[2] Francis Fukuyama, *The end of History and the last Man*, Free Press, 1992, 418 pp.
[3] Samuel P. Huntington, *"The Clash of Civilizations?"*, www.foreignaffairs.com, Summer 1993

It seemed certain that it would take many years to overcome the collapse of the Soviet system. First there was the Boris Yeltsin era and then the accession of Vladimir Putin.

In the 2000s, Russia experienced a new economic trajectory, notably boosted by the sharp rise in commodity prices. At the same time, China was experiencing very dynamic and sustainable economic growth, even though the Western world was not very concerned about China's performance at the time, because it was convinced that such economic performance would not be sustainable, and that China would soon encounter obstacles. Finally, just as quietly, it was in the 1990s that the world began to hear about al-Qaeda, a terrorist organization determined to attack American interests.

On September 11, 2001, the international community was shocked to learn of simultaneous attacks on U.S. soil. These deadly attacks left a lasting impression... and a turning point in contemporary international relations. First, the American ultra-domination was suddenly shaken. Second, a new adversary had appeared on the global geopolitical landscape: Islamic terrorism. Third, 9/11 was the trigger for wars waged in the name of democracy and the fight against terrorism. In other words, these military interventions were to lead to what Francis Fukuyama thought.

Two decades later, it appears that military interventions could not lead to the victory of democracy in either Afghanistan or Iraq. On the other hand, Islamic terrorism was raging in the meantime in several regions of the world. It contributed to maintaining a climate of terror and socio-political instability. In the same way, some states were to experience an economic emergence or make a strong comeback on the international political scene, which would rather give reason to the multipolar and multi-civilizational vision as described by Samuel Huntington. The international community of 2021 is unquestionably multipolar and gives rise to a clash of thoughts in which nothing indicates that democracy will ultimately prevail.

The clash of civilizations is even more perceptible when political messages run counter to Western wishes in terms of political and economic vision. When the Western world denounces China's actions towards the Tibetans, the Uighurs or Hong Kong, Beijing does not give any importance to these criticisms except to remind that everything that happens on its national territory will not be subject to any external influence. China does not intend to give in to any Western demands or requests because it feels strong enough to oppose or refuse any foreign demands. On the other hand, it intends to continue its political and economic progress with its own vision. This means that it will not move towards a political transition to a democratic approach of governance. Chinese objections to Western criticism are partly about the opposition that international actors are now voicing to Western standards.

In this sense, the world is indeed fragmented since there is no single thought or standard that is being imposed on all. The wars waged in the name of democracy, respect for human rights or the fight against terrorism have not only shown the limits of a paradigm vaunted by the West, but above all have contributed to widening the gap in thinking between Western civilization and other civilizations. Indeed, Westerners have often been criticized for intervening in the field for reasons that the locals cannot justify, let alone validate. This is how the dialogue has become progressively tense with certain states, particularly since the attacks of September 2001 and even more so since 2003 with the operation to dethrone Saddam Hussein in

Iraq. This last point is crucial to understand the feelings of the surrounding countries, since the Iraq war was decided based on a big lie: the alleged weapons of mass destruction. However, this did not prevent an international coalition led by the United States to intervene in Iraq, to sow discord and to generate polemics about the conditions of detention of prisoners, such as the famous affair of humiliations perpetrated in Abu Ghraib, the occult affairs concerning the defense of American economic interests such as Halliburton or Blackwater, and so on. There are many other reasons why the Western world has seen its prestige, credibility, and legitimacy decline in certain regions of the world. The Western world is criticized for having generated wars, spread socio-political chaos in several countries while failing to solve local problems... and lastly to opt for the withdrawal of any form of presence as soon as it is admitted that the socio-political situation is definitively beyond its control.

On the other hand, it is also accused of intervening while ignoring the socio-political reality of the targeted regions as well as the local culture. Finally, many voices are raised against the feelings of amalgam or assimilation emanating from the Western world. In fact, we should rather consider a bad Western communication. Thus, foreign political leaders denounce, within the wars undertaken in the name of democracy or the fight against terrorism, an underlying idea that suggests that these same people would be accomplices or supporters of authoritarian regimes or terrorist organizations... This is obviously not the case. Political leaders risk their lives to stand up against terrorism. As for the battles waged to spread democracy, some do not hesitate to point out that their country has a unique political culture.

Unlike in the 1990s, there are now many critics of the political vision as defended by the Western world, especially since the wars unleashed in the name of the standards promoted by the West have led to lasting local and regional disorders that do not seem to be on the way to being resolved. For all these reasons, the clash of civilizations seems more topical than ever and is likely to intensify in the years to come because the fight against Islamic terrorism is not about to end. As for civilizational oppositions, they will progressively become more assertive and China is the best example of a civilization that intends to move forward without worrying about Western, and particularly American, criticism or demands.

Towards a new paradigm of the world economy?
The fight against climate change generates numerous debates on the consequences on the environment and on the world population. Although the official discourse of public and private decisionmakers tends towards a mobilization to promote the tools to prevent a worsening of environmental deterioration, the international economic reality comes up against another reality concerning the consumption habits to be changed. Thus, energy consumption is one of the nerve centers of the global reflection. The main idea is to propel clean energies to the forefront, so that they can replace fossil fuels, whose high consumption contributes greatly to greenhouse gas emissions. However, oil consumption is not programmed to disappear from the global energy landscape any time soon. The energy transition will take time, probably several decades, while the international scientific community (the IPCC in particular) is constantly reminding us of the urgency of making an immediate energy change.

The challenge for the international community is all the greater because global warming is impacting many densely populated regions, starting with coastal areas. The world's habitable surface will tend to shrink and hundreds of millions of people will have to leave the land they currently occupy. This will necessarily have an impact on the regions that will be targeted by these future climate refugees. These migratory waves will be of a different kind than those that began in 2015 (Syria, Iraq, Afghanistan, or Africa) or in 2021 following the return of the Taliban in Afghanistan. The reception of refugees is a matter of debate, particularly in Europe, where not all EU member states share a single vision of refugee reception. Some are categorically opposed to it. Beyond the societal impact, the fight against global warming raises the question of the means and mechanisms to be promoted to obtain significant results and to engage in a sustainable trend of decarbonization of the world economy.

There is a big difference between what is desired and what is achieved. Scientific reports continue to deplore the poor results as they point to continued environmental degradation. In April 2021, the International Energy Agency (IEA) revised its forecast for global oil demand for the current year to nearly ninety-seven million barrels per day. [4] This recovery in global demand for black gold is explained by the fact that the year 2020 has seen an unprecedented decline in demand due to the occurrence of the Covid-19 health crisis and by the slowdown in economic activity in many countries, especially major oil importers. The revision of the IEA is justified by the publication of the conclusions of the International Monetary Fund which forecasts a strong increase in world GDP in 2021 and 2022 (6% and 4.4% growth respectively). [5]

In short, the recovery of economic activity, which has not yet reached pre-Covid levels, favors oil

---

[4] *"L'AIE revoit à la hausse ses prévisions concernant la demande mondiale de pétrole en 2021"*, atalayar.com, April 14, 2021
[5] *Ibid.*

consumption. The correlation is close: there is a link between economic dynamism and oil consumption. This has been observed with China. Its spectacular economic development has been accompanied by a sharp rise in its oil needs. In other words, although many clean energy projects are being promoted around the world and major hydrocarbon producers are increasingly turning to renewable energies, it is to be expected that global oil demand will not decline significantly in the short term. The decline in demand in 2020 was a consequence of the Covid-19 pandemic. This decline was therefore accidental and not expected to be part of a lasting trend. As for the traditional oil and natural gas producers, they are now seeking to produce more to optimize their revenues in a hydrocarbon market where trading prices are struggling to stabilize above $70 per barrel for Brent crude oil, one of the world's major oil trading references.

If a quick summary were to be made, one would have to consider first the US-China opposition. Similarly, the Biden presidency will do what is necessary to move closer to the EU and thus re-establish a new political alliance that was altered during the Trump presidency. Consider Russia, which has tumultuous diplomatic relations with Europe and North America. Moscow is undoubtedly a foreign power that counts in the landscape of international relations. In addition to security issues, we must not overlook the economic reality of many countries that are clearly not yet ready to make a significant change in their national economic model. We are thinking of hydrocarbon producers. Many of them are experiencing lasting economic difficulties because of an economic model that is too focused on oil and gas sales. This model works well when exchange prices are high and therefore favorable to them. However, many of them have opted for an over-reliance on this sector of activity for which a barrel of black gold has not been traded above $100 for a decade... while some are obliged to sell the barrel above this threshold to ensure their budget balance. The current selling prices are obviously not of this kind. The consequences are numerous, including for the richest. The Saudi Crown Prince is forced to "modernize" Saudi society because Saudi Arabia must reduce its public spending and promote a private sector that will require foreign investment. But it is on this precise point that Riyadh and other capitals are likely to encounter a major obstacle: convincing investors.

The oil states that have based their economic model on the rents of black gold have exposed themselves to other dangers, including social instability. As for the political regimes, they are sometimes authoritarian or do not offer the guarantees sought by investors. The case of Saudi Arabia is telling in that this conservative monarchy is seeking to diversify its national economy and intends to undertake ambitious economic reforms. On the other hand, it is experiencing internal turmoil within the ruling family as well as among its national population, which is suffering the consequences of its over-reliance on Saudi Aramco. Recently, Saudi citizens have been paying taxes as well as for services that the state used to provide free of charge. The unemployment rate is rising. As for the sustainability of the regime, this will depend on several factors: will the Crown Prince be able to impose his authority smoothly once he is installed? What will be the evolution of the geopolitics of the Middle East and the Persian Gulf, while the rivalry with Iran will not disappear any time soon and the regional crisis areas are as numerous as they are long-lasting? The list of questions is not exhaustive, but these few questions show that the problems are multiple... and that it is understandable that a country such as Saudi Arabia takes refuge in a sure value: hydrocarbons. It is not surprising that OPEC has expressed a desire to raise its production targets.

However, it seems inescapable that states suffering from "oil dependence" will have to find solutions that will lead to the diversification of their national economies. In the meantime, they are taking refuge in an activity they know and master, which once ensured their wealth, but these are natural resources that are now being "fought" by the international scientific community as well as by states that consider it urgent to actively engage in an energy transition. In a global spirit of competition and rivalry on the international scene, it is to be expected that new economic models will emerge and that, in view of the complexity of rivalries within international relations, they will become a real weapon to establish political and / or economic domination. ESG criteria are part of this category of weapons with strong influence.

International relations now partly shaped by ESG criteria
As indicated in the previous section, a new global economic model will gradually be put in place, even if we should not expect a revolutionary phenomenon. It will take time for change to take place, but ESG criteria will certainly help to ensure this evolution. For the first time, criteria based on ethics, morality and, more generally, on a humanistic approach, are becoming reference elements for favoring or not financing projects. Green finance tackles different evils that are harmful to humanity, whether it is the obvious deterioration of the environment, social and societal issues, or governance. Green finance promotes virtuous economic actors and will on the contrary sanction those who do not respect the desired conditions of collaboration. In principle, the idea is good since it defends the general interest and seeks to combat any form of abuse or drift that also harms individual rights and freedoms.

However, beyond the virtuous dimension of these criteria, it must be considered that there is no such thing as a perfect society and that, consequently, it will be necessary to define the criteria that will make it possible to evaluate the feasibility of an investment opportunity based on ESG criteria. It is therefore necessary to determine evaluation criteria that are as neutral as possible. This is not the direction of our thinking. In this section, the main idea is to show that the gradual and increasing appearance of ESG criteria in the global financial sector has all the qualities needed to become a key player in international relations.

Green finance will certainly play a central role in gradually shaping the new global economic model. First, we think of the fossil fuel sector. This sector of activity is indeed designated as one of the most harmful for the environment and the preservation of life on Earth. This is the reason why most of the major players in the hydrocarbon sector have opted for energy diversification. Many are now promoting renewable energies. However, this will not make the hydrocarbon market disappear any time soon. It is important to be pragmatic and to consider that the resources allocated to the promotion of clean energies remain largely insufficient to allow them to completely replace fossil resources. There is therefore a production problem, but also a problem of competitiveness since the production costs of fossil fuels are lower than those of photovoltaic or wind energy.

Any holder of financial capital has power. However, this statement must be qualified: there are different levels of power, but an economic actor, whoever he may be, with a large amount of financial capital, will have more chances to be heard and to obtain satisfaction. The example of Qatar can be considered since never has such a sparsely populated state been designated to organize a soccer World Cup.

Similarly, this small emirate has managed to resist diplomatic and economic pressure from Saudi Arabia and other Arab states in the region. Without its economic wealth, it is very likely that Doha would never have been awarded the 2022 FIFA World Cup or that the Qatari capital would have been forced to give in to Saudi demands at the height of the diplomatic crisis. Thus, the holder of financial capital is in a position of strength vis-à-vis the one seeking financing. Moreover, one of the subtleties of contemporary international relations is that states are not necessarily at the heart of the major issues. Private companies have become major players in international relations. As far as ESG criteria are concerned, it is the financial sector that will see its influence grow as the motivations or refusals to invest are dictated by political reasons. States are obviously not disappearing from the list of influential players in international relations, but other players are gaining influence. In other words, the great game of international relations will become even more complex with the power games played by public and private actors.

Private actors have become as powerful as states because of their market capitalization or because they manage huge funds. Their opinion or position counts in major decisions. They are now able to influence governments. This is notably the case of GAFAM and their databases, which are of great interest to governments. Investment funds and other financial actors also have considerable power, since they are appreciated by other economic actors seeking financing and are exposed to refusals based on evaluations made regarding ESG criteria. However, we understand that the political dimension of a refusal must not be dismissed when countries are directly designated by financial actors to refuse investment. This is notably the case for Russia and China.

As soon as investment funds communicate in this way, one must perceive a motivation that is not without a political dimension. Considering the postulate that green finance will see its power of influence grow in the coming years, it is appropriate to think that this new deal will influence the new global economic model. Once again, it is more prudent to speak of a transition rather than a revolution, as the process will take time and the industrial sectors or others that are blamed for their polluting impact will not cease their activity any time soon. Rather, they are considering an evolution like the oil and gas giants who are now turning to renewable energy with no immediate intention of ending their oil or gas production activities. However, this situation will disturb international relations insofar as the gap may increase between the dominant players (those who hold the financial capital) and those who will be forced to respond to their demands. It is in this sense that ESG criteria will succeed in imposing themselves as one of the most influential actors in future international relations.

Conclusion

The world is changing. It has always been in a state of flux, but there are events that have led to radical changes. These have usually occurred at the end of a war, a major political or diplomatic crisis. If the economic dimension was never disconnected from these crises, it was never considered as the major element leading to these brutal evolutions. Contemporary international relations are not changing because of war, even if the fight against international terrorism has had an impact. Since the attacks of September 11, 2001, the United States and its Western allies have intervened in several areas where operations have not led to the expected results. At the same time, the economic rise of China has definitively reshuffled the cards of a paradigm of American ultra-domination for more than a decade, at the end of the Cold War, in terms of both hard and soft power. While the United States remains a dominant power in the international arena, the gap that separated it from other state powers has narrowed considerably with the rise of China. The latter has emerged as the most formidable adversary feared by Washington. The opposition is real and seems set to last.

In this clash of titans, a military confrontation would constitute an immense danger for the whole of humanity, which is why such a scenario seems unlikely, although it should not be ruled out. It is more likely that military intimidation will be part of the daily routine of this confrontation without the situation tipping over into the irreversible. In other words, hard power is brandished to make threats, but it is on other grounds that the real confrontation will take place. The ESG criteria are undeniably part of the terrain on which Washington and Beijing will seek to weaken the adversary.

ESG criteria are in many ways a weapon with destructive potential for the actor who holds the rules of the game. As already mentioned, the outbreak of a military conflict between the United States and China cannot be ruled out if military intimidation occurs. An escalation of tensions can occur at any time and be beyond any form of rational control... unless there is a unilateral or bilateral will to do so. However, it is more likely that the two belligerents have an interest in fighting on other grounds. The military dimension remains a classic means of seeking to dissuade the adversary from resorting to arms when the forces involved have equipment and logistical means that could threaten life on earth, and it is desirable that no crisis should lead to the outbreak of military hostilities. However, the Sino-American rivalry must be seen in this light: the United States intends to maintain its economic and military leadership, while China obviously wants to become the world leader.

China is more determined than ever to reach the top. It is in a hurry to get there. Hong Kong is a perfect example. The former British colony has seen its destiny change with more than a quarter of a century to spare. Beijing has decided to do so, and despite international criticism, nothing has stopped it from going ahead with its plans. This shows how sure China seems to be of its strength. It is still the only state power that can categorically refuse the United States, with the possibility of retaliating without exposing itself to overly restrictive sanctions. By way of comparison, Russia regularly opposes the Western world but is penalized by sanctions. China has a superior force. This has undoubtedly contributed to the rise of green finance in the international financial arena. If we defend the postulate of an unlikely military conflict between Washington and Beijing, the economic confrontation will be fundamental.

In international relations, a golden rule is naturally imposed: seek to weaken the opponent. In this case, the economic health of any actor in international relations constitutes a strength but also an Achilles' heel. In a global environment where new technologies reign, the weakening of an adversary can be carried out at a distance, without having to provoke a market dysfunction to generate or impel a damaging economic crisis. In a matter of moments, a remote, sneaky, and unexpected attack can strike an enemy target and cause considerable damage. Cybersecurity has a definite future... as do ESG criteria, which can at any time lead to the refusal of investments in the name of ethics or principles for which the scope of definitions remains relatively vague.

In the past, never has a comparable financial "principle", erected in the name of "responsibility", been conceived with a view to sanctioning deviant or disrespectful actors of new standards imposed by a dominant power. Secondly, it is obvious that international relations have never been so critical because of the growing weight of the technological threat. It is true that the Cold War was a technological confrontation insofar as the idea was to show the adversary significant advances in the field of armaments or the control of the atom. This reality still exists with the difference that there is no longer any need to communicate about inventions or innovations: anyone can feel threatened at any moment; all actors may find themselves the victim of a cyberattack. Digital technology has undoubtedly influenced the evolution of international relations. It is possible to destabilize or neutralize an adversary from a distance. In this sense, a new world order is being established since the traditional means of hard power are now being challenged by new technologies. Therefore, the Sino-American confrontation will rely on these new technologies as well as on moral weapons for which the dimension of the power to sanction an adversary must not be overlooked.

Each era has its dominant actors and is accompanied by major advances in discovery or innovation. In history, traditionally, a dominant state actor was dominant for several centuries. For the past two centuries and the industrial revolution, everything has evolved at a lightning speed with technological inventions, the reality of international relations, the world's addiction to natural resources, political thinking, and so on. Since the 19th century, the general evolution of politics and the world economy has been marked by speed. The more time has passed, the more the speed factor has been decisive. During the 20th century, this factor has been even more decisive since the power games have especially marked the end of empires and situations of domination that have not been as durable as in the past. Ideologies have had a definite impact on international relations, as have the imperatives of consumption. Natural resources have never been consumed as much as they were during the 20th and 21st centuries.

As for power games, two wars on a planetary scale have profoundly modified international relations. Never have military conflicts had such an impact and mobilized so many human and other resources. Globalization has never been so intense. International relations are clearly influenced by large-scale phenomena, in this case global processes. Demographics, growing consumption needs and other factors contribute to shaping the international political and economic reality. In addition, technology, and especially new, advanced technologies, are also playing a role. All of this contributes to the creation of an omnipresent climate of anxiety, for which the capacity to cause harm is considerable. Thus, the intense consumption of certain natural resources raises questions about the consequences on the environment. Scientific advances, particularly in the field of armaments, mean that the weapons developed have an ever more powerful destructive potential.

Ultimately, it is the world's political and economic governance that is now suffering from this situation. The means of pressure, intimidation or dissuasion are growing in intensity while any information, rumor or cyberattack can be deployed and disseminated in record time. Although the list of exposed dangers is not exhaustive, the reality of contemporary international relations is implacable: empires are no longer made to last. The hegemonic domination of the United States in the 1990s is now being strongly challenged by China. It is in this context that green finance has appeared, although it was theorized in the 1980s when the Cold War was still dominating international relations. Since then, the East-West confrontation has ended, giving way to an unprecedented American hegemonic domination... which was short-lived since the 2000s marked a new turning point with the irruption of new disruptive actors: Islamic terrorist organizations. Usually, wars were fought between states. Contemporary wars no longer involve only states. As for the "weapons" aimed at weakening the enemy, they are diversifying. The use of some of them can have irreversible consequences and threaten life on Earth. It is therefore logical that other "weapons" are designed to strike in other ways. Green finance is one of them. In the same way, during the 20th century, oil was the natural resource with the greatest power of influence. In the 21st century, the desire of certain states, led by the United States and the EU, to make an energy transition towards the gradual decarbonization of the world economy will have a major impact on international relations, since the influence of oil on world politics and economics will decline. Oil was a central element, or at least present, in almost all the major political and economic crises of the 20th century. Again, this is an argument for a major change in international relations.

The latter are undergoing a major evolution since the power relationships are changing. Technology (and more precisely new technologies) is becoming increasingly important and certain global processes (global warming, growing demographics, wars, and so on) will encourage the displacement of populations. In other words, on a large scale, other problems will arise and will constitute factors of socio-political destabilization. Thus, the paradigm of the nation-state will once again be at the heart of political and societal issues. It is already subject to numerous debates within the EU, a geographical space in which member states do not share a unanimous vision of how to manage migratory crises. Two broad categories of states can be highlighted: those open to controlled immigration and those that refuse all forms of immigration.

The main problem is that, in view of the global and contemporary problems, the migration phenomenon is likely to increase and concern hundreds of millions of individuals in the coming decades. This means that the national vision, or rather the conception of the nation, will undergo changes that will confront the two great perceptions of the nation as presented by Ernest Renan or Johann Gottlieb Fichte. In short, the debate will be re-launched on an open vision of the national approach and based on the collective will to live together or to tend towards a more clear-cut approach based on common characteristics presumed to contribute to the constitution of a nation.

If we go further in our thinking, large waves of migration may also call into question the multi-civilizational approach developed by Samuel Huntington. In other words, if the nation-state is not to be called into question, the French approach to the nation is the one that should theoretically best consider large waves of migration, but there is still a considerable gap between theoretical thinking and the reality on the ground. When in 2015 the European continent faced a great migratory wave from Asia and Africa, far-right parties had the wind in their sails in several EU countries... and not only since 2016, as the United States elected Donald Trump as 45th President while Brazil is led by Jair Bolsonaro, a far-right politician, since 2019. In a state of economic well-being, far-right parties are generally less sought after by voters. The problem arises especially when a national society is experiencing economic or other difficulties. In such cases, that is when populist leaders are most likely to be heard and listened to. Their discourse usually revolves around accusations, denunciations and the obvious: leaders are incompetent, immigration is the cause of many ills, etc. Populist speeches are based on an unchanging logic, but one that manages to raise the awareness of the nationals who are contesting or who wish to express their anger towards the decisionmakers of their country, whose positions they do not share. A great wave of migration in the Western world will certainly have an impact on the countries concerned by the reception of migrants, whatever the reason for the migration (war, climate, etc.). If there is no economic well-being in the receiving countries, the vision of the nation that will win the voters' favor is likely to be the one advocated by Fichte in his time. More generally, global processes should not be underestimated in the approach to international relations, as they will certainly be influential factors. The fact remains that the landscape of international relations will continue to evolve and to be confronted with problems that will require upstream consideration. The latter will have to be done in such a way as to avoid a flooding effect that could lead to undesirable effects.

The new world order is not going to be established solely because of the rivalry between the United States and China. This dual confrontation will certainly be a driving or central factor in the evolution of international relations, but as indicated above, there are other issues that must be identified and considered because they will inevitably have an impact on international relations. In sum, when we raise the question of the future occurrence of a new world order, the answer is that international relations are in a state of permanent evolution combined with an acceleration phenomenon. As already explained, since 1945 and the end of the Second World War, the international community has undergone profound changes with the emergence and confirmation of the Cold War for four decades and then the collapse of this dual rivalry to end up with the overwhelming domination of a state power that has never known its equivalent in history. At the beginning of the 1990s, American domination was such that it was unthinkable that it could be seriously challenged two decades later. The gap between the United States and the other states of the international community was immense. In sum, the world order evolved according to one-off events and other much more lasting situations that gradually shaped the new competitive reality in the world.

The attacks of 9/11 were a turning point in the international relations of the 21st century. In addition to the fact that American power was struck from within, symbols of power were targeted: financial power was struck with the air crashes against the World Trade Center. As for the attack on the Pentagon, it symbolically hit the American hard power. These tragic events revealed the American vulnerability to this type of attack, but they also triggered a new interventionist vision: the hunt for terrorist organizations and their supporters. It was expected that these attacks would not go unpunished, but when military operations were launched in Afghanistan in 2001, it was not foreseen that they would continue for two decades and that they would ultimately lead to the most feared scenario: the return to power of those who had been driven out at the beginning of the 2000s. For twenty years, the reality on the ground in Afghanistan and Iraq has shown the limits of American and, more globally, Western military power. Western standards have been seriously undermined by the inability to pacify areas in which the Western world intervened to fight terrorism and ensure and support the process of nation-building. The chaotic withdrawal of American troops from Afghanistan is the latest chapter in a long and failed intervention. The chaos in Afghanistan and

Iraq has undermined American leadership, while at the same time other states are emerging at great speed.

First, China can be mentioned, since it has succeeded in building up a formidable economic force in a short time, which has also enabled it to optimize its political power to the point that Beijing is happy to communicate its intention to challenge American economic domination. To a lesser extent, Russia has experienced a rapid resurrection from the legacy of the breakup of the USSR. Moscow experienced an economic upswing in the 2000s due to the rising trade prices of raw materials that the Russian capital exports in large quantities. President Putin quickly showed his political ambitions on the international scene and did not hesitate to maintain tumultuous diplomatic relations with the United States but also with the EU. Several political crises occurred between Moscow and the Western world, which led to a strategic rapprochement between the Russian capital and Beijing. If we cannot speak of a Sino-Russian alliance, it is more accurate to speak of a shared vision of not giving in to Western demands or requirements.

The new world order corresponds more to a world disorder since international relations are driven by multiple poles. Without provocation, we refer to a disorder to underline the growing level of uncertainty surrounding a future that is increasingly difficult to predict or anticipate through major trends. These famous heavy trends blur the tracks. Thus, although the world is multipolar and the US-China rivalry is set to become the great confrontation of the 21st century, any means of intimidation or deterrence can change the course of events at any time. The world's major military powers are developing secret weapons programs, and sometimes communications are made on the subject to send a message to the adversary.

In July 2021, Russia communicated about the development of a new hypersonic missile that it calls an invincible weapon. This is just one example. Everyone is striving to develop new weapons with ever more powerful and potentially destructive defensive or nuisance properties. We must understand the political messages. For several years, President Putin has been talking about a multipolar world. Between the lines, he indicates his refusal to recognize a unipolar world dominated by the United States. Secondly, by multipolarity, he is inducing a competition to the American-Western domination that is of quality but also in quantity. In other words, it implies that the United States must consider Chinese power differently, but also Russian power. This is a minimum, since other state powers will be able to sit at the table of the world's great decisionmakers or dominators in the future, both in terms of hard and soft power. There is therefore an international reality as follows:

- The weapons developed are increasingly powerful by the main dominant military powers.
- The economic gap between the United States and China is narrowing.
- Certain global processes will reshuffle the cards: climate change will have an impact on the phenomenon of migration, while the world's habitable surface area will tend to shrink. Demographic issues, employment, access to natural resources, etc. are all phenomena to be considered as factors of future tensions or crises.
- The destabilization or socio-political instability in certain regions will increase the power or influence games within the dominant powers, such as the Afghan crisis.
- New means of pressure are now part of the reality of international relations: new technologies can impact a public or private actor at a distance, while green

finance relies on undefined standards that can counteract important financing needs.
- The energy transition is going to play a crucial role with the programmed decline in the weight of oil in the world. Other resources will replace oil in the future, and it seems that green finance could become a real substitute for black gold as an instrument of power or intimidation in the world.

Here are a few points that tend to indicate that the new world order is increasingly uncertain due to factors or trends that are being put in place but that are making relations between states and / or integrating private actors more complex. Private companies have considerable economic means that sometimes exceed those of states. The world is evolving at great speed. This is an undeniable fact. As for the US-China rivalry, it should not obscure the fact that there are many other institutional and private actors who can at any time disturb or disrupt international relations, for a variety of reasons. All of this contributes to the fact that the balance of international relations will become more precarious and increasingly uncertain.

Election and undecided results
November 2020

November 3, 2020: the long-awaited day has finally arrived! Americans, depending on the legislation of the state in which they reside, had the choice of several ways to vote. They could vote remotely as they had the possibility to go to the polling stations, despite the Covid-19 pandemic and the two hundred and thirty thousand deaths it caused in the United States. Until the last minute, Donald Trump and Joe Biden ran their election campaign to win over the undecided electorate. The Democratic candidate had an overall advantage in voting intentions according to the polling institutes, but everyone remembered the blow of 2016 and the defeat of Hillary Clinton when her victory seemed to be a foregone conclusion. If the outgoing President has never spared his efforts to fight a campaign despite a coronavirus contamination, his crisis management of the pandemic has been reproached with the economic consequences induced. Moreover, he has often been attacked for his perception of the health crisis, which he has allegedly underestimated and whose real seriousness he has obviously not measured. The Covid-19 has hurt him.

However, before this health scourge hit the entire international community, Donald Trump had a generally positive record, particularly in economic matters, where his famous slogan *"America first"* has largely favored American companies and jobs. Certainly, some election promises have not been kept, such as the construction of a wall on the border with Mexico, which was to be financed by Mexico City according to Donald Trump, but which has not been built, except for a portion of a few dozen kilometers... financed by American funds. The election campaign took place in a particular climate, very stormy, with its share of polemics and violent attacks by the opposing camps against a backdrop of social and racial tensions: the Americans mobilized massively and more than one hundred million of them voted, which is a record but at the same time a precious indicator of the general state of mind that reigns in the United States. The nation's population is as divided as the political elites, who are engaged in a struggle that looks like a real war.

As D-day approaches, fears are high in Uncle Sam's country where unusual scenes have been witnessed with the erection of barricades in front of many shops and offices in major cities due to a perceived risk of tensions between Republican and Democratic supporters, as if it was already anticipated that the outcome of the vote would necessarily lead to a non-recognition of an electoral defeat. In other words, the situation is very worrying and social calm will only come about if the losing side is wise enough to acknowledge its electoral defeat... unless there is an obvious malfunction in the vote count, a hypothesis that would not favor political and social appeasement.

The U.S. presidential election (as well as the election of state representatives, senators, and governors) has long been identified as the major event on the international political calendar for the year 2020. Everyone was waiting to see who would win the public vote, either the measured Joe Biden or the elusive Donald Trump. The voting intentions published by the polls announced a relatively large gap in favor of Joe Biden, but after the vote and the announcement of the first results, it turned out that the gap was not as big as announced and that, if not heading for an easy victory, the Democratic camp would have to face defeats in states where a success for Joe Biden was expected and would contribute to secure a majority of the electors. The problem is that not all states have the capacity to announce results on the same day, because for some states, it will be necessary to take the time to count the votes cast by mail, which are postmarked to validate a vote. Some Americans waited until November 3 to cast their ballots and some votes will not be known for several days while all the mail is received.

At first, results will be announced but not final. Finally, in every presidential election, it is customary for the loser to call his or her opponent to concede defeat. This did not happen between Donald Trump and Joe Biden. Worse, each of them has publicly announced their high chances of success. All these conditions do not favor a peaceful outcome. It is indeed to be feared that the results will be contested, that the Federal Supreme Court will be seized in fine, but also that there will be social outbursts. This scenario was feared, and it is unfortunate that the chances of it happening are increasing as the counts show a small gap between the two main candidates in the election. There is reason to be concerned about this turn of events. The real problem is not the organization of the election and the conditions in which it was held. The real problem is the hatred between the main political forces and the desire to destroy the opponent through the most incompatible affairs required for a President of the United States of America.

Confirmation of a persistent malaise
Should we be surprised by this turn of events? The answer is no. All the clues pointed to what was going to happen on November 3. The tone had been set by the incumbent President, who for several weeks had been announcing that he would contest the results if he lost the election, citing possible malfunctions in the organization of the election. This announcement could be considered as a means of intimidation addressed to the Democratic camp, but it turns out that there was no attempt at bluffing: Donald Trump had persuaded himself to contest the results. He

could not lose! Is this the inveterate determination of a sore loser known for his public facetiousness and cheating when playing golf? No. The answer is obviously no. In doing so, he is simply highlighting a persistent problem in the United States: since the beginning of his term of office, his governance of the state has been severely disrupted by numerous cases brought by the Democrats whose sole purpose was to compromise Donald Trump. He had to be pushed out by any means necessary. This is how the affair on the alleged Russian collusion broke out, which was cleverly orchestrated for the sole purpose of associating the name of Donald Trump with Russia, a country accused of having used cyberattacks in 2016 to disrupt the presidential election at the time. The goal was to show that Donald Trump had benefited from benevolent Russian help in finding ways to beat Hillary Clinton. Since then, the trouble has never stopped.

Donald Trump has been the subject of a lengthy FBI-led investigation due to suspicions of collusion with Russia. When the federal police director was fired in May 2017, a special prosecutor was appointed by the Department of Justice (DoJ) to continue the investigation initiated by the FBI. This investigation was taken over by Robert Mueller, himself a former boss of the institution, whose work continued for nearly two years until his conclusions were handed over to the DoJ in March 2019. He could not provide evidence of Trump-Russia collusion, something for which the main suspect then trumpeted a message denouncing an arbitrary witch hunt, a hoax or other qualifications denouncing the incongruity of the case. The problem for Donald Trump is that the Democratic camp, not very satisfied with the conclusions of Special Counsel Robert Mueller, based some interpretations in which they thought they perceived a cryptic way to denounce suspicious links between Donald Trump and Russia. This led to Robert Mueller being questioned by two congressional committees in July 2019 to clarify obscure points in his conclusions. Clearly uncomfortable, he did not provide any evidence for Democrats to pursue Russiagate to an even greater level.

The day after the Mueller interview, Donald Trump made a phone call to his Ukrainian counterpart, during which Volodymyr Zelensky was asked to launch an investigation into suspicious activities of the Biden family in Ukraine. Several weeks later, a congressional investigation was launched, which led to the impeachment proceedings for which the Senate eventually rejected the impeachment of Donald Trump. All this history only exposes the tip of the iceberg. The evil is much deeper. Yet these few lines of explanation show the determination of the Democratic camp to find the legal means to have Donald Trump impeached or to push him to resign.

We have followed the evolution of the case very closely. Above all, we have understood that the Democratic camp has relentlessly insisted on harming Donald Trump, but by means of procedures that have clearly transgressed the rules of federal law. The scandal is immense because the original Operation Crossfire Hurricane launched by the FBI was hardly justifiable but was legitimized by maneuvers that have no legal basis. Time has helped to forget the conditions that influenced the launching of the operation, but it was based on information allegedly communicated by Joseph Mifsud, a Maltese university professor, to George Papadopoulos, then a member of Donald Trump's election campaign team, that Russia had many compromising emails against Hillary Clinton. It was never proven that Joseph Mifsud had communicated this information, although he has always defended himself from having communicated this to George Papadopoulos. However, this is what triggered the

FBI investigation and what became the surveillance and espionage operations against him.

For a long time, Donald Trump had understood what was happening but was systematically blocked by the desire to communicate, which could turn against him on the grounds of obstruction of justice or abuse of power. The accusations against him were numerous, sharp and should have brought him down. Considering this, how can we imagine for a moment that he would not want to fight with an opponent who was at the time of the facts the Vice-President of the United States? This is the reason why everything was organized to denounce the presumed connections of the Biden family with countries such as Ukraine, Russia, or China. Despite the denunciations, nothing has been able to prove until now that candidate Joe Biden has no legitimacy to represent the Democratic camp for the presidential election. Therefore, he has the right to seek the American presidency. We know, however, that the election battle is likely to be disrupted by old grudges that will be expressed through a challenge to the results.

Foreseeable problems
On Wednesday, November 4, the counting continues, one after the other, with each state announcing its election results and consequently the political color for which the designated electors will vote, in most cases. The Democratic candidate has long been in the lead. At the end of the day, with the announcement of the victories in Wisconsin and Michigan, there was no doubt that Joe Biden would become the 46th President of the United States of America. He still had to win six more electoral votes to secure the decisive majority. While four states were still in the process of completing the counting of votes cast, it appeared that Nevada and Pennsylvania would give the Democratic camp a victory.

For several months, Donald Trump had announced his intention to claim electoral fraud because of the votes cast by mail. This could be interpreted as a form of pressure on the electorate not to vote for the Democratic candidate, an anti-fair-play attitude, and a great provocation as only he knows how. In short, such an announcement could have been a bluff. Yet, if he has not kept all his campaign promises during his term, he has rarely bluffed when it comes to attacking his detractors, those who have done their best to weaken him during the four years he has been in the White House. Clearly, Donald Trump does not want Joe Biden to succeed him because of the continuing disputes that have plagued the relationship between the outgoing President and his Democratic foes, who have consistently brought out compromising cases.

It is therefore necessary to read the situation at a double level. Between the desire of some to fight and the normative rules, the consequence is that the actions taken are not for direct reasons but indirect one. Donald Trump will try to find a way to make his opponent accountable to the American justice system for the activities involving his son Hunter with different countries. With this logic in mind, it is not surprising that he intentionally decided to disrupt the final vote counts to delay the declaration of Joe Biden's final victory. In the Republican camp, there was optimism that Donald Trump would win the election, but it turned out that the congressional elections, however close they were, gave the Democratic camp a slight advantage. Similarly, there was a high level of popular mobilization for this presidential election, with a higher turnout than in previous presidential elections. The absentee ballots cast, according to the polls, gave the Democratic candidate an advantage. When he decided to address the American people on November 3, after the first states had given their electoral verdict, there was only one alternative: either Donald

Trump would publicly acknowledge his defeat, or he would engage in a dangerous tug of war with an uncertain outcome. He opted for the second possibility.

This choice was not surprising after all. It was however feared. While not having reached the climax of an internal political and institutional crisis, Donald Trump's attitude is reminiscent of that of a sore loser, but one who intends to rely on the irregularities he denounces to have the legitimacy to appeal to the Supreme Court of the United States. First, it is not certain that he will win the case. Second, he is pushing his country further into crisis because such a decision carries a high risk of social tensions between Democratic and Republican supporters. In absolute terms, this decision to challenge the validity of the election is an anti-democratic act, unless the facts support it and there is a case to challenge the validity of the election. For the sake of the United States, it is desirable that the New York businessman did not use an ultimate ploy without a well-founded reason because, in this case, based on law, he would only be replicating what he has so often denounced in his opponents since 2016. If he deliberately disrupted the vote count when there was no legitimate reason to do so, that is an attack on democracy. Unfortunately, everything that happened was predictable. It was to be expected that Donald Trump would not accept defeat in the election: he had already announced it, claiming that if Joe Biden won the election, it would mean that there had been fraud somewhere. The accusation is extremely serious and could lead to an even greater social fracture than the one the United States has already experienced for several months. To put it another way, Donald Trump is playing with fire by not wanting to acknowledge his defeat if by any chance it took place under impeccable conditions. The problem lies in his fierce desire to do battle with the former Obama Administration and to prevent one of its members from being democratically elected. Once again, this is a very dangerous game because if the election was conducted normally, the designated winner must be Joe Biden.

Who is right?

One must admit that the Trump Administration has not succeeded in bringing past scandals to light as it would have liked. Moreover, the media should not be held responsible for this. However, the media played into the hands of the Democratic camp when the Russiagate and Spygate affairs resounded in the American political and media landscape. There was this relentlessness during which any compromising information about Donald Trump made the headlines, especially for anything related to alleged Russian collusion. Despite the Robert Mueller's findings that could not establish a link that led to a suspicious election victory for Donald Trump in 2016, doubts persist as information has become public that the Steele dossier (the dossier, spearheaded by a former British MI6 agent, Christopher Steele, sought to show that Donald Trump and some of his close associates were linked to prominent Russian nationals) was fanciful and that the process that led to the launch of Operation Crossfire Hurricane had a suspect legal basis. The origins of the investigation remain unclear, but the Mifsud case never came to light as it might have. This probably played a role in Donald Trump's decision to engage in legal wrangling over the validity of the November 3 election, although it does not make it legitimate.

Donald Trump had personal reasons for wanting to create a scandal around matters concerning the Biden family. He claimed to have information that would raise questions about how Hunter's son was able to prosper with such ease in Ukraine or China. The purpose of the maneuver was to damage the public image of the

Democratic candidate, but also to find a way to start a legal process that might have resulted in Joe Biden's ineligibility. In our opinion, this was the goal. Because of the lack of time or because the collection of information did not lead to the obtaining of material and irrefutable proof, Joe Biden was able to run his election campaign despite the bad reputation that his opponent wanted to give him. The problem for Donald Trump is that his management of the health crisis was poor, and he was probably punished at the ballot box for this reason. In fact, the difference may have been made by voters who voted Biden for the sole purpose of opposing Trump. That said, as the political and institutional crisis seems to take shape more and more, we keep in mind that the Trump Administration, despite some declassification of classified information about the Biden family or Hillary Clinton, could not take down its major asset, Joseph Mifsud, because of the likely Democratic reaction that would have been to challenge such a maneuver under suspicion of interfering in the presidential election. Our question is this: if Joe Biden were to be officially inaugurated President of the United States on January 20, will Donald Trump have pulled out his Mifsud trump card by then?

The prevailing schizophrenia is that Joe Biden was democratically elected by the American people, while the question of his legitimacy as a candidate for president arises before that. This is the heart of the matter. In this case, it is a repeat performance. In 2016, the same question could be debated about Hillary Clinton. Since then, despite some information made public, nothing has been able to officially establish that the former Democratic candidate was the architect of a scheme created from scratch to compromise Donald Trump with a dirty deal linking him to Russia. The declassified evidence was not sufficiently probative to warrant prosecution. It is on this point that we bounce back to the Joe Biden case. At the time of the facts, he was the Vice-President of the United States. A declassified handwritten note shows that former CIA Director John Brennan had briefed President Obama on a particular situation that was to trigger Operation Crossfire Hurricane. The question is: was Joe Biden briefed on what was going to happen and obviously concern Donald Trump?

There are many questions. Many people are still convinced that things happened in 2015 and 2016 did not respect the normative and ethical rules that must guarantee the proper functioning of democracy. These were covert operations that were carried out for electoral purposes and with the aim of favoring the candidacy and then the election of Hillary Clinton. This is what the Mifsud case tends to show. This man was not catapulted into the wake of George Papadopoulos by chance. The goal was to trap him, to introduce him to Russian nationals to support the thesis of a Trump-Russia collusion. It was necessary to give weight to this official version by showing that members of the close guard of the Republican candidate had secretly established links with Russians. This is what happened. But this was never publicly accepted or acknowledged. George Papadopoulos has since spoken before Congress and published a book [6], but it has never been possible to do the same with Joseph Mifsud, the latter having mysteriously disappeared since November 2017. His testimony could have undoubtedly given a different direction to Russiagate-Spygate.

The invocation of electoral fraud
This strategy is outrageous in Europe. The incumbent President is using every possible means to

---

[6] George Papadopoulos, *Deep State Target: How I Got Caught in the Crosshairs of the Plot to Bring Down President Trump*, EverAfter Romance, March 26, 2019, 288 pp.

demonstrate electoral fraud in several states, including those where candidate Biden won the electoral votes. The number of legal actions has increased, and it is precisely this point that worries many European observers: Isn't Donald Trump obstructing the democratic functioning of American governance? The answer is simple. It is affirmative if there are indeed abuses on his part. It is negative if electoral fraud is proven. Three days after the election, with several states still to report results, Joe Biden looks set to win most of the electors who will elect the winner of the 2020 presidential election in December.

The social climate is extremely tense. In several large cities, supporters of both sides are taking to the streets, with pro-Biden supporters denouncing an anti-democratic move by Donald Trump and pro-Trump supporters giving wide credence to the theory of electoral fraud. The overall climate is all the unhealthier because American society appears increasingly divided and the greatest risk is that of a loss of control of the situation if it degenerates. This is perhaps the scenario secretly hoped for by Donald Trump. On November 5, the state of Michigan denied his request for an appeal of a claim of voter fraud. Meanwhile, Joe Biden opted to ease tensions by communicating in a cautious manner. Indeed, if he recalls that he is confident of winning the election, he does not intend to enter a communication battle with Donald Trump, whose rhetoric he knows will be offensive and denunciatory in the extreme.

From our perspective, this is an extremely perverse situation. The incumbent President is trying to find the right legal mechanism to challenge the validity of the election in several states. If this were to be proven, it would be normal for him to assert that right. The problem is that he is suspected of wanting to confiscate power, of not recognizing his electoral defeat on the basis that he could not lose and that in such a case the defeat could only have come from fraud. It is dangerous to think in this way because if there is an abuse of the accusation, the whole American democratic edifice is potentially threatened by a drift of power. Donald Trump is known for his facetiousness, his whimsical and volcanic character, but he must not abuse his powers to impede the proper democratic functioning of institutions. Once again, he may have good reason to suspect electoral fraud, which he did not fail to mention several weeks before D-day when Americans were allowed to vote by mail.

In absolute terms, Donald Trump must be sure of himself and make sure that he has good arguments and information to denounce electoral fraud. This is a very serious accusation. If he lies, he will have wrongly set himself up against the democratic institutions of his country. Furthermore, he will have opened the door to future challenges in the upcoming presidential elections. This bad experience would be very damaging for the United States, as rarely has a presidential election been so heated in Uncle Sam's country. On November 5, Donald Trump gave a televised address in which he once again denounced the "robbery" of the election from him. He bitterly regretted that this did not respect the will of the American people, convinced that without fraud he would have easily won the election. Such a statement prompted MSNBC to interrupt the live broadcast of the speech, while CNN opted to broadcast the entire speech... before a star anchor from the network criticized the speech as an attack on the national democratic balance.

In any case, this election was marked by a significant fact: the non-recognition of an electoral defeat against the background of suspected fraud. This is a traumatic event in more ways than one, because in essence, one political camp clearly tried to prevent the rival camp from winning in a democratic manner. Either Donald Trump is taking a huge risk by raising unfounded suspicions with the possibility of inducing institutional and social disorder based on lies, or the accusation is founded and then proven, in which case we should also expect serious political and social disorder. The big loser in this election is democracy. It is even more regrettable that this scenario was, after all, expected: Donald Trump had clearly announced his intention to contest his electoral defeat in the event of his defeat by arguing that he could not lose without resorting to cheating. He kept his word. He lost, did not concede defeat, and engaged in an unprecedented legal battle to try to prove what would ultimately seal the United States' entry into its most serious political and social crisis since the Civil War. While the results have not yet been announced, a famous quote from Abraham Lincoln's Gettysburg Address must resonate in the minds of many Americans: Democracy is *government of the people, by the people, for the people.*

A strategy of contestation to better rebound on past cases?

By struggling as he does, Donald Trump undoubtedly intends to send a message to his fellow citizens: the Democrats are cheaters and are therefore unworthy to lead the United States of America. Once again, everything must be based on the truth: if there has been a lie or fraud, it must be proven beyond a shadow of a doubt, and there must be material evidence that definitively validates this hypothesis. If he fails to do so, he puts his country at risk by seeking to retain political power that would have been won democratically by his opponents. This is the reason why the United States is going through a political crisis of frightening intensity, but one that has nevertheless been underlying for several years, since the official inauguration of Donald Trump in January 2017. We have the impression that the challenge to the election results is a way of denouncing the relentlessness set in motion by the Democrats with all the political and other affairs that have been denounced for the sole purpose of pushing him towards impeachment or resignation. The Democratic plans have been rejected, including the impeachment proceedings in the Ukrainegate scandal.

President Trump may have his own reasons for wanting to go after his Democratic opponents, but if Joe Biden were to win the presidential election on a regular basis, he would have a hard time justifying all the appeals filed based on suspected voter fraud. The cure may be worse than the disease. Donald Trump is driven by a deep desire for revenge against those who have done their best to disrupt his presidential term. However, care must be taken not to strike back by jeopardizing national democratic institutions. This will probably be the most difficult to argue if no electoral fraud is detected. Indeed, we suspect a strategy that consists of showing by any means that the election did not take place under perfectly transparent conditions and that irregularities were found. On the other hand, it is indeed possible that there were errors during the counting of the ballots, but this does not necessarily imply fraud, i.e., an intentional attempt to cheat. Thus, the charge of fraud is strong and dangerous: it suggests that the Democratic side deliberately cheated. This is an attack on democracy. Donald Trump is going to have to prove adverse culpable intent. This will be difficult to prove.

Our feeling is that Donald Trump is trying to buy time to advance a case in which Joe Biden would be directly incriminated, in connection with the apocryphal affairs of his son Hunter. Clearly, his idea is to show that the Biden family got rich in suspicious or even corrupt conditions. Is he capable of invalidating an election if a candidate is caught up in legal cases whose quality of the offences could deprive him of any chance of being elected if the facts reproached are sanctioned? We believe that this is the strategy that Donald Trump is seeking to develop. If our hypothesis is correct, we do not know what the American justice system would interpret in such a case. Is it simply possible to have a presidential election invalidated retroactively? This has never happened in the past. Yet this is the path that the outgoing President seems to be taking: he obviously wants to make Joe Biden accountable to the federal justice system for alleged past offenses that could deprive him of his civil rights if he is convicted.

From our perspective, Donald Trump does not intend to stop at the conditions of the Biden family's enrichment. We see this as a loophole that could lead to even more serious accusations. We believe that Donald Trump wants to reopen the Russiagate-Spygate case. In his eyes, this is the best way to show that the Democratic camp has played with the rules of federal law and endangered the democratic balance of the country. We do not know if he will succeed, but we are convinced that if this is his true intention, the American socio-political crisis would be far from over. Worse, it would only be the beginning, with a high risk of social unrest and the fear that the situation would eventually spiral out of control by federal authorities.

By embarking on a policy of challenging the validity of the election results, it is feared that Donald Trump has in fact embarked on another battle, but one that he will have difficulty justifying based on a denunciation of electoral fraud, if indeed there was any fraud. If he starts such hostilities over unfounded suspicions, the damage done will be lasting. We were convinced that he would not accept the scenario of an electoral defeat, because he is willing to denounce the actors who have harmed him during his entire term, to denounce the people of the former Obama Administration who, according to him, engineered this unbelievable Russiagate affair when Joe Biden was still the Vice-President of the United States. For this reason, we are convinced that Donald Trump will open a new crisis in the American political landscape, whether he eventually admits defeat in the election or not, as his desire to make a big public announcement has become irrepressible.

The call to declassify sensitive documents

On November 8, while some elected Republicans recognized Joe Biden's election victory, Donald Trump still refused to accept what had been publicly announced by the US media. He intends to continue his battle on two fronts: first, to open a maximum of legal recourses to try to have a hypothetical electoral fraud recognized; second, a call to declassify numerous documents that we presume to be independent of the November 3 election, but which would refer to old cases that he intends to reopen to find a way to compromise Joe Biden and his allies. The maneuver is not without its dangers. It seems to us that his intention is to revive the Russiagate affair and to seek to demonstrate that he was indeed the victim of an attempted conspiracy in the 2016 presidential election, which he eventually won. The Russiagate (and later Spygate) case was unique in that an investigation was launched against him to determine whether there were any established relationships with Russian nationals that would have allowed him to win the election. The investigation was initially opened by former FBI Director James Comey and then continued by the DoJ with the appointment of an independent investigator when the latter was fired by Donald Trump in May 2017. Special Counsel Mueller's findings were delivered to the DoJ in March 2019. Since then, the Russiagate case has seemed destined to never come up again...

There are two approaches to this scandal. First, the one that validates the official version, the one communicated by Attorney General William Barr, who publicly stated that there had been no Trump-Russia collusion demonstrated. This version resulted in a triumphant reaction from Donald Trump, who openly claimed that there were no charges against him, and that the Mueller report showed that he had been the victim of an odious attempt to compromise. Second, there is the version that William Barr did not fully account for the Mueller report and managed to keep secret parts of the report that would incriminate Donald Trump... Former FBI agents are also convinced that their former boss (for twelve years) managed to uncover murky relationships between Donald Trump and Russian businessmen that could have affected the 2016 presidential election. In fact, according to some, the President-elect, through his relations with wealthy Russian nationals, became an agent of Russian intelligence services... In any case, the protagonists agree on one point: the attitude denounced in the opponent undermines the democratic foundations of the country. As far as the contextual analysis is concerned, it is a fact: without determining who is right or wrong, the accusations are so serious on both sides that there are obviously liars who endanger the democracy of the United States of America.

We do not know what Donald Trump intends to do or declassify, but we assume that he intends to return to this affair that is so painful for him and for which he keeps reminding us that he was the subject of a campaign of surveillance and espionage that he intends to denounce by declassifying documents that could confirm his claims. The question is how much leeway he will have and whether he can declassify everything he wants. Indeed, as far as the FBI investigation is concerned, it is not a public criminal investigation but a counter-intelligence case that is classified. He has never ceased to hammer home the point that the conditions of the investigation were full of elements that did not respect the rules of law. In this case, if he succeeds in declassifying what he wants, we would not be surprised to see the name of an important person who worked in the surveillance and espionage operations reappear in the person of Joseph Mifsud, the Maltese academic who got in touch with George Papadopoulos. His alleged statements about information indicating that Russia had tens of thousands of compromising emails against Hillary Clinton, once reported to the FBI, had contributed to the opening of Operation Crossfire Hurricane. If Donald Trump reopens this case by declassifying information, he will reopen a Pandora's box while the DoJ awaits the conclusions of Special Counsel John Durham who is investigating the first investigation which was led by Robert Mueller. Clearly, if Donald Trump does not obtain satisfaction in the legal appeals initiated to invalidate the results of November 3, it is very likely that he will fall back on the Russiagate affair for which he will aspire to give a new impetus by bringing new elements to what is already known ... knowing that in line of sight, he is targeting the former Obama Administration and its former Vice-President, Joe Biden. This maneuver is undoubtedly the last card that the outgoing President will be able to play before having to proceed with the transfer of power in January 2021. Until then, the debates are likely to be animated in the United States. Everything seems to indicate that Donald Trump will not shy away from any option that he deems appropriate to allow him to continue his presidential experience. It is to be hoped that the reasons given are legitimate and well-founded. If they are not, there is no need to explain how undemocratic they would be.

What options does Donald Trump have?

On November 9, Attorney General William Barr authorized investigations into the conduct of the presidential election but said there was reason to suspect voter fraud. On the same day, Donald Trump fired his Secretary of Defense, with rumors of a rift between the two men, especially when the Pentagon chief refused to use the armed forces at the president's request during racial tensions in several major cities. Donald Trump seems determined to go all the way. He is seeking to challenge the validity of the election by any means necessary, while the unwavering support he expected is dwindling, with many calling on him to concede defeat. The more he is challenged, the more he steps onto a slippery slope, opting for controversial decisions. He does not intend to concede victory to Joe Biden without using every possible ploy to try to retain executive power. If no one can prove that there were improper maneuvers deliberately carried out to impact the election, Donald Trump will forever remain the man who did his best to retain power without any intention of respecting the democratic foundations of his country. If there is no evidence of fraud, he will be seen as the one who jeopardized the nation's democracy, even though he has always criticized his opponents for violating federal law in the previous presidential election. If he has any evidence, now is the time to bring it to light.

Donald Trump is a fascinating character insofar as he is divisive in the extreme. Some people adore him while others hate him, but this man has an exceptional quality which is his power of conviction. He is driven by an extraordinary sense of communication, capable of turning around situations that are apparently the most unfavorable to him. He is known to be an inveterate liar, someone who shows little empathy and whose only obsession is the defense of his personal interests. He refuses any hint of defeat, only victory matters, and that's how he dazzled the American electorate in 2016 with his promise to make America *great again*. His speech hit home. A wealthy businessman who has experienced ups and downs to the point of near bankruptcy, he never lets himself be defeated despite all the attacks he has been subjected to. He has an amazing confidence that some would call arrogance. Donald Trump is arrogant, but this excess of personality has appealed because he is seen as a leader, a man who points the way forward. *"Trust me and you'll get to heaven."* This is a slogan he could have used. He never seems unsettled, always ready with a scathing, offensive response. He does not know the defensive position. When attacked, he responds like a bulldozer clearing a field of rubble. He is known to be a liar, manipulative and untrustworthy. Yet, his speech continues to make an impression and convince many Americans that their President is indeed the victim of a ruthless adversarial cabal that would almost make him a martyr.

It is important to put all of this into perspective. Donald Trump has probably lied a lot throughout his career. Arrogant, manipulative, and unsympathetic, he certainly is. He is a sore loser, no doubt about it. Is he right to go on a wild goose chase to show that the Democrats planned voter fraud? The answer is no if he has no way to prove it. Yet he has a masterful option to try to reverse what now appears to be an extremely compromised situation: a return to the Russiagate-Spygate affair. However, there remains a big unknown: considering the hypothesis that he has sufficient evidence to show that his political opponents have indeed used illegal means to compromise him since 2015, could this lead to a cancellation of Joe Biden's electoral victory if it were to be shown that he was linked to illegal operations? In other words, in a context where a candidate has been recognized as the winner by the media but not by his direct opponent, where numerous legal actions have been opened to disrupt the counting of votes or to try to have the election invalidated in several federal states, would an old case be likely to render a man ineligible while the election has already taken place and he is clearly the winner? This has never happened in the past. Of the forty-four former Presidents, thirty-five left office smoothly with a democratic transfer of power, eight died during their term, and only one, Richard Nixon, resigned before being subjected to a humiliating impeachment procedure after he realized that his cause was no longer tenable. As for Donald Trump, his challenge to the election results is unique in national political history. His strategy seems to be to capitalize on what has never been before American jurists and to engage in a novel tactic that will lead the magistrates to consider a legal issue that has never been anticipated by the rule of law at the federal level.

Conclusion

The United States is amid a serious political crisis, perhaps the most serious since the Watergate scandal that saw President Nixon resign, a unique act in national political history. The crisis is undoubtedly more serious than that of the 1970s, perhaps the deepest since the Civil War. The allusion is not exaggerated: we are witnessing an astonishing and unexpected context despite the promise made by Donald Trump, that refusing any recognition of final victory of Joe Biden. He did! Rightly or wrongly, he did what no one had dared to do before him, in the name of democracy. Yet it is democracy that has been considerably undermined because whatever the result, whether there was fraud or not, there is bound to be a liar who has damaged the democratic foundations of the country.

Either a political side deliberately cheated, and this is in fact an attack on the national democracy; or Donald

Trump does not admit to losing and goes out of his way to make a hypothetical or even fanciful case of electoral fraud to prevent his democratically elected opponent from becoming the 46th President in the history of the United States of America... In such a case, if there is no evidence of electoral fraud, this would also be an attack on the national democratic foundations. However, beyond these political issues on the background of democratic concerns, all this comes at a time when American society seems more divided than ever. Donald Trump knows this and is relying on this situation to create even more disorder and discord where Joe Biden is calling on the American population to remain calm. The wisdom of the old Democratic lion is remarkable, and he is no doubt aware that his rival will never give up without being certain that he has exhausted all existing means to achieve his ends. He will only withdraw from the race once he has been let down by all and finally convinced that he can no longer reverse the course of events as he would like. Donald Trump's ethics are no doubt questionable. He never does anything like the others, always ready to break the rules of law with a certain talent to ensure that he is never caught by the federal justice system. His whimsical personality does the rest: he is allowed to do anything and justify anything even if it creates commotion and indignation. He is Donald Trump, a facetious character who amuses as much as he annoys by his disconcerting, volcanic and unpredictable character.

All the appearances seem unfavorable to Donald Trump, his accusations of electoral fraud have very little chance of succeeding and being proven... if there was even a proven attempt at electoral cheating. There is always the possibility of a twist of fate that would support the accusations of the incumbent President, but this hypothesis seems unlikely. Donald Trump is throwing his last bit of strength into a fierce battle to try to retain his political power, which he does not intend to transfer easily to Joe Biden. There is still one option, admittedly very hypothetical as to the expected result, which may disturb this period during which the United States is supposed to be preparing for a transfer of power: the reopening of the Russiagate-Spygate case. Donald Trump is not a choirboy, that's for sure. However, he has good reason to refer to what he calls an attempted coup d'état that almost happened in 2016. At that time, there were maneuvers aimed at compromising him. The Steele dossier, the meeting in Trump Tower in New York and other unsavory files on morality have damaged the image of this man who has never been discouraged and who has always taken the fight to him.

As far as Russiagate is concerned, he was the object of attempts to destabilize him, which were to lead to a compromise. Mechanisms were put in place to trap him. This is what happened with Professor Joseph Mifsud, the man whose name was widely reported when the Papadopoulos affair broke in the media. This former campaign adviser to Donald Trump found himself in a media whirlwind as he was questioned by the FBI and then arrested by federal police for lying to it. Lying is a serious offense in the United States. George Papadopoulos had referred to a strange university academic who had made a confidence to him about the fact that Russia would be in possession of many emails compromising Hillary Clinton... This mysterious messenger was Joseph Mifsud, and his name was then exposed in the media in October 2017. A few days after this media exposure, the main person concerned disappeared. This was the beginning of a long soap opera about the man's past, his suspicious relationships and the hypothetical reasons for his sudden disappearance. At first, he was reported missing, then rumors of his death appeared, increasing the mysterious dimension surrounding the man who was not destined to become famous in this way... However, this man undoubtedly embodies the demonstration that Donald Trump intends to use to definitively prove that he was indeed the victim of a relentless cabal during his entire presidential term and that his opponents have indeed transgressed the rules of law to compromise him and push him to resign or be impeached. Joseph Mifsud is the shadowy figure who can expose what was really going on when Donald Trump publicly stated his intention to run for president in 2016.

On November 10, tensions seemed to be rising with a new media episode marked by Fox News' voluntary interruption of a press conference given by the White House spokeswoman as she began her speech by expressing her belief in illegal voting and fraud in the election. On the same day, it was Secretary of State Mike Pompeo's turn to make a comment in which he expressed confidence in Donald Trump's transition to a second term as President. In short, one week after the big election day, the outgoing President does not admit defeat and is multiplying his legal appeals, while no evidence has yet come to confirm his accusations. However, he still has support even if some Republicans prefer to acknowledge the electoral defeat of their political camp and accept the victory of Joe Biden.

For his part, the man who is presented by the media as the winner of the presidential election is continuing his considerate communication, devoid of polemical remarks and for which he continues to speak of a transition that will take place smoothly, as if to reassure the United States. This is probably a good attitude, as many doubts remain because no official institution has yet recognized Joe Biden's official victory. In other words, if no proof of electoral fraud could be established, it does not mean that there was none. It is quite possible to imagine the scenario that brings confirmation of Donald Trump's accusations of election irregularities. However, if he were to be successful, we do not know how long the political crisis would last. It would be up to the Supreme Court to rule that the election was invalid, which would be a first case for a presidential election. Moreover, such a decision would only be the prelude to a new bombing operation against the opposing camp. In any case, the fight promises to be fierce between Republicans and Democrats and Donald Trump will play his last trump cards to try to reverse a situation that is unfavorable to him.

The call to declassify everything remains mysterious in that it is a very clear message as to the intentions but unclear as to the nature of the documents targeted. As mentioned above, we are convinced that this refers to the dark Russiagate affair and that it is about to take new twists and turns. It may also be that he intends to declassify other documents that we do not know exist and that tend to reveal compromising content for Joe Biden and the former Obama Administration. From our point of view, if any documents were to be made public, they would be related to Russiagate and Spygate because Donald Trump's major asset remains Joseph Mifsud. For the time being, we know that the US Administration has a lot of material relating to the life of this man, his professional connections, his missions, his political and intellectual affiliations, etc. Special Counsel John Durham continues his investigation while no one knows what he has discovered or uncovered. We thought for a while that he would report before the presidential election. This is not the case. Instead, we are driven by one conviction: the November 3, 2020, election will forever be the one that symbolizes a great political divide in the United States and has led to a surreal scenario with respect to the democratic values that Uncle Sam's homeland so strongly defends in the world. This is damaging the image of the United States in the world as well as its credibility on the international political scene.

76

Oil prices and the US presidential election
November 2020

With one week to go before the big election day in the United States, even though some voters have already cast their ballots electronically, most polls show Joe Biden as the winner, but all of this is taking place in a particular climate in which it would be a mistake to underestimate the ability to reverse a trend unfavorable to Donald Trump. It is important to remember the scenario of the previous presidential election, when Democratic candidate Hillary Clinton was assured of victory before she realized that her opponent had finally managed to win more electors from states than her. The incumbent has not yet lost, even though the trends that are most apparent are those of a Democratic victory. It is perhaps because of this uncertain climate that the oil markets are once again going through a lean period and that trading prices on the international markets remain low, equivalent to $40 for a barrel of Brent and around $38 for WTI. The US election is obviously not the only political element explaining this uncertainty weighing on the financial markets, but it is nevertheless a major contributor, since this election event is the one that will crystallize the world's attention the most, between the many people hoping for a Democratic victory and the much smaller number of people who would not be unfavorable to a re-election of Donald Trump.

The November 3 election is undoubtedly the great global political event of the year 2020. This electoral campaign was marked once again by the exacerbation of political tensions where polemics and personal attacks took precedence over the presentation of real political programs. The tendency was to sabotage the image of the opponent and all the tricks were allowed. In short, the final duel between the two main candidates in the election resembled more a pugilistic fight than a heated political contest. Certainly, Donald Trump and Joe Biden do not share a common vision for the political and economic future of the United States, but the Covid-19 health crisis was undoubtedly a disruptive element that no one expected just one year ago. Since then, several hundred thousand Americans have been affected by the disease, which, according to the WHO, has killed several million people worldwide. Donald Trump's management of the health crisis has been widely criticized by his Democratic opponents, who have seen him as incapable and even overwhelmed by the gravity of the situation. Meanwhile, one would almost forget the consequences of Covid-19 on the world economy which, since China, the original home of this form of coronavirus, began to see its economic dynamism slow down due to decisions on sanitary measures aimed at trying to contain the spread of the virus as quickly as possible, has rapidly reached an international and global dimension.

The major consequences of the economic slowdown were initially manifested in a decline in Chinese demand for oil. On a global scale, China has quickly become one of the major players in the world of oil market due to its growing demand for its domestic needs, which have exploded over the last two decades to the point of making it the world's largest importer of black gold. Given the country's demographics and industrial needs and considering the very dynamic growth rates of the economy for almost two decades, China has contributed to the evolution of the world oil markets, whose global demand has been growing ever since, reaching a global production of one hundred million barrels per day before the Covid-19 health crisis. As noted, China is considered the original home of this disease, which in a matter of weeks has gone from an epiphenomenon to a global pandemic.

China quickly took the measure of the sanitary problem and decided to confine the population of the administrative region of Wuhan for several weeks to limit the risks of propagation of this coronavirus. The problem is that this decision occurred while many Chinese tourists, unknowingly infected by the virus, were able to travel, especially in Europe, where new infectious outbreaks were quickly created before becoming severely affected areas. The global human toll is very high. On a global scale, it is now estimated at several million deaths if statistics could be correctly established due to major difficulties in the census methodology. For example, many deaths in the homes of victims could not be reported as being directly related to Covid-19 while these people could not be seen by medical personnel.

Nearly a year after the outbreak of this pandemic that has truly impacted the global economy, the US presidential election comes at a time when many countries seem to be at a loss to manage the health and economic crisis. Many predicted that there would be no second wave of Covid-19 and no re-containment... However, this is the scenario we are heading towards. The first wave of containment had a significant impact on many national economies whose main concern was that they would not have to face such a second wave. Many took on large debts to cope with the crisis and to try to keep their national economies afloat, which suddenly became very uncertain. Meanwhile, one of the consequences of this dual health and economic crisis management was a considerable drop in the world demand for oil, while at the same time, the drop in production was not equivalent to that of demand. The logical consequence was an overabundance of black gold on the trade market and the inevitable fall in prices.

In March 2020, OPEC+ (the alliance that includes the OPEC cartel and other non-OPEC producers, led by Russia) tried once again to agree on a global oil production cut to stop a downward spiral in prices that would eventually suffocate the national economies of many producing countries dependent on hydrocarbon sales. As prices fell at a rapid pace, a disagreement arose between Saudi Arabia and Russia. The result was an unexpected reaction by Riyadh, which provoked the international markets by embarking on an aggressive price policy that caught everyone off guard. The maneuver was to put pressure on Moscow to review its refusal to reconsider an effort to reduce its domestic oil production. Russia did not panic, even though trading prices kept falling and were therefore unfavorable to it. The Saudi gamble was all the riskier as the desired effect was initially achieved... but probably too much. The exchange prices collapsed to the point of becoming dangerous for the economic balance of the Wahhabi kingdom, considering moreover that no one knew how to stop the bad spiral that had just taken shape. The decision endorsed by Crown Prince Mohammed bin Salman was fraught with consequences in a global context where the Covid-19 was then seriously affecting Western economies. These same countries, importers of oil for the most part, characterized their difficult management of the health crisis with decisions concerning a strong slowdown of industrial activities and more globally economic, which resulted in a significant decrease in the demand for oil.

The infernal loop had just taken shape. The main unknown was how long the Covid-19 would last on the planet. Soon, the idea was to work on the development of a vaccine that would counter the spread of the pandemic. The problem is that such a challenge requires time, something that the international community was sorely lacking at the time. While several countries were competing to be the first to find the formula for a miracle vaccine, it became clear that hopes for the rapid commercialization of a vaccine with uncertain properties should not be pinned on the market. It was then that the WHO communicated the information that we had to accept that the pandemic would not be eradicated before 2022, while a few weeks later, during the United Nations General Assembly, Russian President Vladimir Putin expressed the feeling that the world economy would not regain its pre-Covid-19 dynamism before 2023 or even 2024... The stage was thus set: the lights were turning red. It had to be admitted that the health crisis would last longer than initially expected and that economic troubles would therefore be inevitable.

It is in this very uncertain context that the American presidential election is taking place, a country that has been strongly affected by the pandemic and that has recorded more than two hundred thousand deaths attributed to Covid-19. As for the cases of contamination, they are of the order of several million individuals. The worst may be yet to come. President Trump was personally infected by the virus, requiring a hospital stay of less than a week, during which time he was twice in respiratory distress. After being released from the hospital, he resumed his electoral campaign, wanting to demonstrate that his strength and determination had been stronger than the disease. Beyond this political communication, the November 3 election raises many expectations and fears. Some fear a re-election of Donald Trump and thus wish a victory for Joe Biden. Others would be more inclined to a victory for the Republican candidate, who is more likely than his opponent to promote a rapid return to a dynamic economy. The problem is that everything remains speculative since no one knows what will happen to Covid-19 if it penalizes the international community through decisions to restrict economic activities and the movement of individuals. It is therefore to be expected that the demand for oil will fall back to the level of April, May, or June 2020. Reduced demand will not encourage the price recovery so hoped for by the producing countries, which are suffering badly from the situation. As for the policy of adapting production to real demand, it also remains uncertain.

We identify the following trend: the risk of an overabundance of supply in relation to real demand is high and could lead to an even more harmful problem for the financial markets: oil storage capacities could quickly be saturated. If this problem were to arise, there is no need to demonstrate the negative effects on exchange prices, which would inevitably tend to fall. In short, the American election symbolizes the major event on which so many expectations are based... which are likely to be disappointed, regardless of who wins. Indeed, the real determining factor does not lie in the final electoral result but in the terrible unknown that remains on the duration and the severity of Covid-19, both sanitary and economic. However, this does not absolve the political environment from also influencing the exchange prices of oil, which appear to be very high in relation to the new trend that is emerging regarding health crisis management.

The limits of the supply and demand paradigm

It is one of the fundamental principles that every student of economics learns during university studies: the price of a good is set according to the supply-demand ratio. When the supply of a good is much greater than its demand, prices tend to fall. Conversely, when demand exceeds supply, prices tend to rise. The exchange price is the result of a fair and balanced compromise between a seller and a buyer who refer to the market trend to finalize their transaction. There are exceptions. A seller may deliberately seek to sell at a price below the market price. Conversely, a buyer may agree to buy at a price above the market price. However, the predominant rule is that of a balance between supply and demand. In this logic, the same applies to all goods produced and traded. Oil should not escape this exception. But the reality of the oil market is nuanced. There is basically a link between the supply and demand of oil to set an exchange price, but the reality is much more complex because it turns out that these very particular markets are subject to speculation whose impact on the prices displayed refers to influences outside the simple oil market.

Oil is unique in that it is a natural resource with considerable influence. It acts as a kind of barometer for the entire financial markets. When oil prices collapse, there is usually an acute financial crisis with global repercussions. The financial markets are constantly concerned about the development of oil prices. When prices collapse, it is not only a simple imbalance between supply and demand that is to be seen, but also exogenous reasons that contribute to a critical influence on prices. The price of oil can thus be driven up by a simple announcement effect that refers to a fear, a danger relating to geopolitical or other issues, to apprehensions concerning production capacity, the transport of raw materials, storage capacity or other concerns that will encourage a speculative effect that will not systematically reflect the reality of the concrete market. In other words, the trading price of black gold is in no way or solely conditioned by simple supply-demand correlations and this is precisely what constitutes a danger for the world oil market.

On a simple announcement effect, prices can go up as well as down. Everything depends on the power of influence or nuisance of the sender of the message. If the fear is unfounded, the financial markets quickly regain confidence to readjust an exchange price more in line with its value based on the supply-demand paradigm. When an oil price crisis is sustained, it must be understood that there is an underlying dysfunction. Since 2016, one must conclude that something is disrupting the black gold market beyond the simple supply-demand relationship. In 2016, that disruption had a name: shale oil. Indeed, the United States embarked on a vast policy of producing unconventional oil that disrupted international markets because in addition to increasing supply on the world market, it turned out that shale oil contributed to lowering exchange prices because of an economic model of exploitation that allowed its producers to sell the barrel at a price much lower than that of conventional oil while making a margin. This caused a disruption of the market, as the other major producing countries did not understand the consequences of the irruption of American shale oil on the world oil market.

After some time of desperately low trading prices for producers needing to sell at much higher prices, they eventually rose to levels between $70 and $80 per barrel during the "best" times for producers. But for many of them, these selling prices were not satisfactory. However, prices were not going to go back up. In 2018, President Trump did everything he could to keep selling prices relatively low to fulfill a mid-term election campaign promise of very low prices for the American consumer. The strategy was a sustained production effort and a willingness to sell abroad to further disrupt the global black gold market. Since then, prices have stabilized at around $60-65 per barrel or below. At the end of 2019, a new phenomenon appeared: the Covid-19. Within a few weeks, what was later reclassified as a pandemic affected the global economy to an unsuspected degree. The first signs of the economic crisis were seen in China when it was decided to slow down economic activity by gradually reducing the demand for oil. This was characterized by the beginning of a supply-demand imbalance, as Chinese demand was substantial and production had not slowed down at the same rate, resulting in a situation of overproduction compared to real demand. This phenomenon was even more striking when the West had to resolve to consume less for the same sanitary reasons as China, while producers could no longer agree on a production policy more in line with real demand. This led to overproduction, which led to another problem: the storage capacity of black gold.

In the introductory section, mention was made of a deep disagreement within the OPEC+ alliance and the unexpected reaction of Saudi Arabia to embark on an aggressive policy on exchange prices to provoke a reaction from Russia... which ultimately did not come. This decision had formidable consequences. This is what allows us to say that the oil market does not depend exclusively on the supply-demand relationship. The Saudi announcement caused a panic that resulted in an abysmal and uncontrollable fall in prices. If the decision had come from a secondary player in the world oil market, the repercussions would probably have been less. In this case, it came from one of the world's three largest producers and involved another member of the world's three largest producers. In other words, the two countries on which the disagreement over production policy to raise prices was based accounted for more than twenty million barrels produced each day in the world. In such circumstances, it was certain that the Saudi announcement would inevitably have a major impact on the supply-demand relationship before it was even apparent. The main problem is that Saudi Arabia had just played a card that it hoped Russia would eventually accept. This did not happen. Moscow did not react to its production policy. Prices collapsed. At first, this seemed to be an advantageous situation for the United States. A month after the Saudi announcement, the United States was forced to react, as the situation also became dramatic for American producers.

A losing Saudi bluff or a stroke of genius?

The feeling that dominates afterwards is that of a thoughtless act. The idea was to force a reaction from Russia that was long overdue and never came. Saudi Arabia had found itself in a very delicate economic situation, as its national economy is largely based on oil sales. The lower the prices, the more they penalize the Saudi economy, which is not very diversified and depends too dangerously on the vagaries of the financial markets. While Russia also depends on sales of its hydrocarbons, the critical point is not comparable. The Russian economy is more diversified. As for the sales prices desired to achieve a balanced budget, they are much lower in Russia than in Saudi Arabia. Moscow knew this. That is why the Russian capital did not give in to Saudi demands. Riyadh's reaction was somewhat desperate if not well thought out. It was a bluff that did not work. More than six months after the event, trading prices remain desperately low, largely insufficient to allow Saudi Arabia to hope for a rapid return to budget balance and to consider its ambitious *Vision 2030* economic development plan with confidence. The Russian economy has suffered from the fall in the price of black gold, but probably not as much as Saudi Arabia's.

At first, the situation suited the United States, which hoped that its oil would find easy buyers under conditions that were increasingly disadvantageous for its competitors. At the same time, while world supply did not decline, demand fell drastically to the point that prices collapsed dramatically. Worse, the exchange prices were no longer able to satisfy the American producers. The situation was out of control as supply far exceeded actual demand. This caused prices to fall. A month after the Saudi announcement, the U.S. market encountered unexpected difficulties: many producers were holding stocks that could no longer be sold, putting the survival of many U.S. companies at risk. In April 2020, trading prices fell to an unprecedented level, to the point of becoming negative: the seller found himself obliged to pay any buyer to offload his stocks as soon as reference was made to the US WTI. This unprecedented situation prompted President Trump to contact Saudi Arabia and Russia to find a solution to the production policy and try to quickly stop the downward spiral that was weakening the national economies of many producing countries. Was the real Saudi goal to force the US to react? If so, the gamble was extremely risky, especially since several months after the event, oil prices had recovered but at a level that was still unsatisfactory for Saudi Arabia.

In October 2020, the exchange prices allowed the American producers who had been able to resist to limit the damage. It is important to understand that the uncertainty surrounding Covid-19 was central to the disruption of trading prices. Similarly, poor institutional communication on the management of the health crisis did not reassure the financial markets. On the other hand, world production of black gold continued to outstrip real demand, leaving many stocks unsold and generating another critical situation, namely that of storage capacity reaching saturation, which could lead to a further fall in prices. The reality is this: with one week to go before the US presidential election, oil trading prices do not reflect the real supply-demand ratio and are maintained at a level that is dangerously high. Explained differently, the slightest malfunction can generate another severe price drop.

Faced with the vertiginous fall in prices and particularly that of the value of WTI, the United States was obliged to intervene, to contact Saudi Arabia and Russia to find an agreement on a reduction in production and to stop a bad dynamic that risked penalizing many producers. It goes without saying that in such circumstances, many jobs were threatened, and some sacrificed. A few months before the presidential election, Donald Trump had no choice but to attempt a delicate maneuver to limit the damage caused to the American oil sector. Since taking office in the White House, President Trump has made no secret of his desire to boost the domestic oil sector by focusing on shale oil production and entering the export market to increase overall supply and allow international trading prices to fall. The lower the prices, the more they were to promote the competitiveness of American producers whose production and operating costs were then lower than those of their international competitors. The problem is that a balance had to be found, low enough to penalize the competition, but high enough to allow American producers to make a margin over the cost price per barrel.

The month following the Saudi announcement was in this sense terrible for the United States. Prices fell rapidly and it seemed that the situation had become unmanageable. It was imperative to find a solution to reassure the financial markets in the first instance and allow them to speculate on a different context in favor of a new stabilization of the supply-demand balance. Demand had fallen sharply, but the reverse was not true for production. It was therefore necessary to urgently readjust this imbalance, for which the risk of sinking into a severe crisis of exchange prices had then considerably increased. The survival of many companies and jobs was at stake in an electoral context that had so far been favorable to Donald Trump, while the

Covid-19 pandemic was beginning to affect the United States, and New York State in particular, heavily. Criticism fell on his management of the health crisis because of an alleged underestimation of the gravity of the situation. The number of victims increased daily, and the President of the United States began to lose confidence. He could no longer afford to allow Saudi Arabia and Russia to maintain their respective but divergent positions and for trading prices to continue to fall dangerously. His intervention then looked like a rescue operation. Indeed, the American oil lobby is among the supporters of the head of state representing the Republican camp. An economic disaster for this strategic sector of activity would have been an additional handicap to manage in view of the presidential election. Therefore, we defend the thesis that the American intervention in the oil markets was the sign of a disavowal that had not been envisaged a few weeks earlier. The strategy then consisted of observing the Riyadh-Moscow disagreement while betting on a weakening of these two countries on the world oil market. Clearly, the difficulties that these two major producers would encounter were to benefit the United States, which could then hope to conquer new international market shares. The calculation was coherent until the price of WTI was impacted to the point of threatening the survival of the national oil sector.

We believe that since the United States has embarked on a frantic policy of producing shale oil, the model is dangerous because it is probably not sustainable. Certainly, the economic model differs from that of conventional oil and has the advantage of requiring less capital investment for a faster return on investment. In other words, by investing in production capacity, the United States can increase its production, influence world supply and, above all, thwart the plans of other producers who need to sell their barrels at a higher price to make a profit. This is how the United States managed to disrupt the supply-demand balance and to pull down the exchange prices. The aim was to make this situation a new and sustainable norm and to disrupt the ambitions of the OPEC+ alliance. This worked until the Covid-19 pandemic upset the global economy and encouraged a sharp decline in economic activity. One of the major consequences was the sharp decline in global oil demand. By maintaining a high production policy, it was to be expected that the world oil market would become disrupted, and its system would be in a state of unprecedented crisis.

In short, the price decline was predictable, but not to such an extent, especially in the value of WTI. What happened in April 2020 with this short, staggering episode of negative trading values should sound like a warning signal for any oil player wanting to assert a growing power of influence on the global market. This is the major lesson to be learned. The American ambition was to weaken its competitors by forcing them to sell their oil at a price that did not satisfy their real economic needs. The gamble was daring and risky, but it seemed to work for a while until the limits of the strategy became apparent.

In general, the American position on the world oil market is very isolated. Every producing country has an interest in selling its black gold at the highest level, to get the best possible margins. American production remains a very small part of total world production. Consequently, it seemed unlikely that a player, albeit dominant but isolated, would be able to influence exchange prices in the long term. The United States managed to do so for a time because international competition had not considered or properly assessed what the introduction of shale oil on international markets would entail, and especially the differential importance in terms of economic model. It is precisely on this point that the United States has bet. Price volatility was less of a burden for US producers if the markets did not get so excited that they reached a state of panic over the oversupply. The latter posed the problem of the capacity to store considerable reserves, which would come up against the difficulty of finding buyers. It was in these circumstances that the American strategy met its limits.

Joe Biden's energy strategy unfavorable to oil

As the November 3 election approaches, polls give the Democratic candidate an edge in voting intentions. Donald Trump has been criticized for his handling of the health crisis, the economic crisis, and racial tensions. Joe Biden insisted on these points to try to influence the electorate not to renew its confidence in the outgoing President. He tried to be less polemical than his opponent and presented a program that goes against Donald Trump's, especially in terms of energy. Beyond this very different approach, the oil markets also experienced a new episode of uncertainty in September and then in October 2020: the contamination of Donald Trump with Covid-19.

It's no secret that if the incumbent is re-elected, he will continue his energy policy, which is focused on the oil sector. This is not the case for the Democratic candidate, who has opted for an energy vision reminiscent of President Obama's. When it was announced that President Trump had been infected with the coronavirus and was hospitalized for several days, fears arose. How was he going to cope with the disease a month before the presidential election? Doubt set in. In addition, it was announced by the medical profession that the President of the United States had twice been in respiratory distress. Although he was given a medical treatment that only the wealthiest can experience, there were many uncertainties about the health of the President, who did his best to show that he was recovering his physical abilities at a very high speed. Thus, he chose to make a highly publicized exit from his hospital room to greet his supporters who were concerned about his state of health, while his final discharge was scheduled for the next day. The purpose of the communication operation was to show that he is a strong man and that he can resume his electoral campaign while not being weakened. The message was addressed to his opponent whom he continues to denigrate by denouncing his age and his "inability" to properly manage the United States for four years in case of victory.

However, despite his fight against the disease, Donald Trump has apparently not convinced Americans who believe that he has largely underestimated the danger of Covid-19 or even that he intentionally withheld information from the entire nation. In other words, the coronavirus contamination probably came at the worst possible moment because, if not a victory in terms of political communication, it has undoubtedly increased the level of uncertainty at the end of the election campaign. This has been felt in the financial markets, which are giving credence to a victory for Joe Biden. In such circumstances, prices could only tend to fall because the Democratic candidate has clearly stated his intention to get the United States off oil. In addition, the U.S. stimulus package is still under discussion, although very uncertain. Tensions between Azerbaijan and Armenia are raising fears of attacks on the Baku-Tbilisi-Ceyhan pipeline and possible disruptions to the transfer of oil to the Turkish terminal... while Turkey persists in its provocative diplomacy which exasperates the Western world. The rebound in the number of Covid-19 contaminations in the world resounds as a guarantee that the demand for oil will be fatally altered and that prices will not rise again in the immediate future. The only positive sign for the oil markets remains the announcement of Chinese economic growth of 4.9% for the third quarter in annual variation. Very briefly, there is little reason to believe that oil prices will recover. Trading prices are likely to be disrupted for several months as the WHO estimates that there will be no eradication of Covid-19 before 2022... unless the announcement of a successful vaccine restores confidence in financial markets.

As for the global geopolitical context, there are many signs of concern due to persistent tensions in the Middle East, the Caucasus and Turkey's ambiguous diplomacy. As for the US presidential election, a victory for Joe Biden would certainly have implications for the US oil sector. In such circumstances, oil trading prices are unlikely to rise in the immediate future unless effective pandemic vaccines are commercialized. A Democratic victory may suggest that the US will seek to reduce oil production in the coming years. Such a trend, coupled with the future eradication of Covid-19, would be a compelling argument for a new dynamic towards rising trade price levels.

Uncertainty around the presidential election
To say that there is a great deal of uncertainty about the future election results is an understatement! On the eve of the election, even if a part of the population has already expressed itself through electronic voting, a process that has raised many questions on the Republican side, the outcome of the vote seems more undecided than ever. The polls continue to give an advantage to Joe Biden, while the methodology of American polling organizations has often been questioned, as in the 2016 presidential election, when Hillary Clinton was declared the winner. However, the Democratic candidate has a lead in collecting most of the electors who will decide the final fate of the election. The two main candidates are throwing their last efforts into a battle that has taken place in a poisonous climate, plagued

by controversy and personal attacks, while Donald Trump has not hesitated to communicate his intention to contest the election results in case of defeat.

We are convinced that we will not know the name of the winner on November 3. There is a good chance that the results will be contested. Even though Joe Biden has publicly announced his intention to accept defeat if Donald Trump wins, it is not certain that he will honor his commitment if he does, because it is very likely that the loser will contest the results, especially because of electronic voting. It is to be expected that new controversies will arise. We understand even better why Donald Trump did his best to get the Senate to ratify his decision to appoint a new judge to the federal Supreme Court, because in the event of a lasting challenge to the election results, it would be up to this court to rule on the validity of the election or not. The Supreme Court is the ultimate judge, the one that will determine whether to invalidate the November 3 election. If this were to happen, it would create a major political crisis in a country where the opposing factions now have a deep-seated hatred for each other and where it will be difficult to reach a wise compromise. For example, the Democrats explain that if Donald Trump is defeated, he would face legal action that could lead to a prison sentence. The same is true for the Republicans, who keep hammering away at the idea that the Biden family will soon have to answer to the federal justice system, not to mention the statements made by people close to the outgoing President, who are hoping for indictments by the Durham investigation against personalities who were part of the former Obama Administration.

The United States is amid a major political crisis of a magnitude rarely seen in the past. Everything seems to indicate that the November 3 election will not be a justice of the peace but the event that will further expose the tumult that plagues national politics. This is currently what appears to be the most likely scenario. However, we are not immune to a reversal of the situation. If we still must wait to know the identity of the President-elect until 2024, we cannot exclude a scenario in which the defeated party accepts its electoral defeat and the controversial affairs eventually subside. This would be the best thing for the democratic exercise of the institutions, because as things stand, the democratic durability of the American system has been severely tested. However, this reasonable scenario seems unlikely, since the rivalries are so great, and the Pandora's Boxes are open. On Monday, November 2, it was not surprising that oil prices continued to fall. Brent was traded around $37 while WTI was traded below $35. This negative trend is linked to the uncertainty surrounding the election and the upcoming results, which are likely to be challenged by the losing side... if a majority is apparent after the votes are counted. This is one reason why we should not expect a rebound in trading prices in the days following the vote. The financial markets can only agree that uncertainty will increase, especially if the election results are contested. This would add even more gloom to the financial markets.

In this time of health and economic crisis, oil prices are a major issue as a sustained period of low exchange prices would have catastrophic implications for many national economies. While there are other factors influencing exchange prices, the US presidential election is undoubtedly the one that will have the most impact on financial markets anxious to understand what course of governance will be taken... if the winner can be inaugurated as president in January 2021. The most credible hypothesis is that of increased uncertainty due to the power struggles between the Republicans and the Democrats, while the Covid-19 pandemic continues to disrupt the international economic balance at a time when many countries are once again deciding to confine their national populations, with all the economic inconveniences that will ensue. As for the oil markets, there is no room for optimism.

Conclusion

The presidential election of November 3 is the major political event of the year. In a generally tense geopolitical climate, everything that happens in the world's leading economic and political power therefore has implications and repercussions for many things. Consequently, any form of fear expressed against the United States manifests itself on the international financial markets. This is part of the speculative game of finance. As for oil, it is even more impacted because the Covid-19 crisis led to a sharp drop in international demand while global supply did not quickly adjust to the reality of demand. This precipitated the decline in exchange prices. In addition, the United States is a major player in world oil. It intentionally disrupted the global oil market by embarking on intensive production of shale oil. This resulted in a new supply because of the choice to export part of the production while US oil could be traded at a lower price than conventional oil. Explained another way, the United States unilaterally decided to change the landscape of the global oil market by weakening competition, the latter wishing to keep trading prices high.

When Donald Trump won the 2016 presidential election, he supported a new policy aimed at boosting the oil sector by championing a climate-skeptic view of the global warming paradigm. Above all, he saw an opportunity for American producers to revive the industry, increase production and win international market share by offering oil that is cheaper than the competition. The gamble paid off, insofar as the exchange prices fell to the point of penalizing the competition while favoring the American producers... and the national electorate. Indeed, this was one of the campaign promises of the 2018 mid-term elections: Americans needed access to cheap oil. The promise was kept. As for the U.S. oil industry, it was experiencing something of a renaissance and thus gave its electoral support to Donald Trump. The latter was counting on this support for the 2020 presidential election, but his campaign plans were disrupted by the onset of the current pandemic and disputes among other major international oil producers. This dangerous combination resulted in a dramatic drop in trading prices.

The economic consequences for U.S. producers were such that when WTI prices turned negative, it was feared that many U.S. oil companies would be forced out of business permanently. Many had to shut down altogether. This contributed to the rise in unemployment, while Donald Trump saw a risk to his re-election: he could not lose the support of the oil lobby. Thus, he resolved to reach an agreement with Saudi Arabia and Russia to boost trading prices and try to limit the damage. Since then, although trading prices have gradually risen back to around $40, the new pandemic and the growing uncertainty surrounding the November 3 election have only confirmed what was already inevitable: trading prices could not be expected to rise again.

If Donald Trump is re-elected, the financial markets can expect him to do his best to revitalize the U.S. oil sector on which he is basing so many hopes for economic success, while conversely, a victory for Joe Biden would tend to reduce the influence of the oil sector in national energy policy. The Democratic candidate would then engage in an energy policy that would be consistent with the one deployed in his time by Barack Obama. The two main presidential candidates are radically opposed on their energy programs. This contributes to the uncertainty in the financial markets, while other factors external to oil are worrying financial speculators. Under such circumstances, the future of oil is a concern.

US oil policy will be perpetuated for another four years if Donald Trump wins or will undergo a major change of course if Joe Biden wins, all of which is part of a logic of uncompromising political warfare in which potential enemies are ready to engage in the most vicious low blows to weaken adversity in all circumstances. If the result of the election were to be contested, there would probably be two big losers: the first would be a challenge to the proper functioning of democracy in the United States; the second would certainly be the oil industry. It is difficult to foresee a new positive momentum in the oil markets in the event of a serious political crisis in the US. If such a crisis were to occur, it would inevitably have a negative impact on all international financial markets, which would be severely disrupted by the uncertainty in Washington and which would immediately be reflected on Wall Street. It goes without saying that a major stock market upheaval in New York would quickly be followed by its effect on other stock markets around the world. However, this is the scenario that seems to be taking shape more and more in the run-up to the November 3 election.

In the end, the Democratic candidate won more votes than his opponent and managed to win more electoral votes. Donald Trump quickly denounced large-scale electoral fraud and launched numerous legal actions to stop the counting of votes in some states and even to invalidate the election. Unless concrete evidence can be provided to justify the fear of fraud, which has not been confirmed by Republican poll workers, there is little chance that the appeals will be successful, although there is a very small chance that the incumbent will win. However, the situation remains very sensitive because the press has recognized Joe Biden's victory, while Donald Trump does not intend to admit defeat. This behavior has logically outraged the world. The New York businessman has been widely criticized: he is accused of lying but also of undermining the democratic foundations of the United States. In this case, if no electoral fraud is detected, it must be recognized that the attitude of Donald Trump has something to question. Quite quickly, several big Republican names disassociated themselves from the presidential position and publicly acknowledged the final victory of Joe Biden. However, everything suggests that the electoral chapter is not definitively closed.

The United States is going through a serious political and institutional crisis. Donald Trump persists and refuses to admit to an electoral defeat for which he is now calling on his Administration to declassify all documents likely to demonstrate past Democratic turpitudes. He does not intend to acknowledge a factual situation for which he would preserve the democratic foundations of his country, convinced that he has been the victim of a vast illegal enterprise to prevent him from continuing his four-year presidential term. As already noted, there are two possibilities. First, his fears are well-founded, and he is exposing a serious assault on national democracy with shameful electoral cheating, in which case we should expect dire consequences for the validity of the November 3 election. Secondly, he is abusing the situation, trying by any means to refuse the transfer of power to a democratically elected man, in which case he is undermining national democracy and exposing himself, if necessary, to legal consequences. In either case, the main victim is American democracy.

By calling for everything to be downgraded, it must be understood that Donald Trump firmly intends to reopen a dark affair for which his opponents are suspected of having broken the rules of law to prevent him from reaching the supreme grail in 2016: the Russiagate. This old case may indeed come out of the closet and bring some surprises. The problem is to determine the legal consequences that this may have, if any compromising elements can be made public with probative force. Until January 20, 2021, Donald Trump remains the President of the United States with the official prerogatives of the national head of state. If he fails in obtaining satisfaction through all the legal recourses initiated to try to invalidate the election results, he will have several weeks left to play his game and to try to bring out old cases for which he will inevitably ask himself the question of determining whether they can have an influence on the validity of the presidential election. Although he has not conceded defeat, Biden has nevertheless acquired most electors who should endorse his election victory before final approval by Congress in January 2021.

The indecision that reigns in the United States is extraordinary insofar as no one has ever contested the result of an election as Donald Trump is doing, while observers doubting the wisdom of such a reaction are in the majority. Such a climate will not help oil markets in the very short term. The latter need to be reassured and Donald Trump does not intend to calm a situation in which he is apparently playing the bad role. He must be careful not to compromise the democratic foundations of his country. Therefore, his protesting attitude is so disturbing and unworthy. Either he is the cheater and liar often decried, or he is indeed the victim of an unacceptable scheme in a democratic regime.

In either case, there will be a scar that will testify to a deep trauma that is shaking American society.

Considering the mess, he is causing, if he were to hand over to Joe Biden, there is little doubt that Donald Trump would quickly see dark clouds gathering over his head: legal proceedings would most likely be initiated against him. Thus, we are led to consider that the battle has only just begun and that his intention to declassify numerous documents is likely to occur to generate even more chaos in an American society that is already very disturbed, as Republican sympathizers had begun to acknowledge the electoral defeat of the man for whom they had given their support. It is to be hoped that Donald Trump does not engage in a desperate attempt to seize power for illegitimate reasons. In such a case, the national socio-political crisis would worsen without it being possible to determine the consequences, which would be dramatic for the survival of democracy.

Joe Biden and the American oil lobby
November 2020

There are lobbies in the United States with which it is preferable for any politician not to confront in an adversarial manner. The powerful National Rifle Association (NRA) is an example. Donald Trump understood this well when he openly advocated that Americans should be able to legally obtain weapons for self-defense, while the country regularly experiences tragic shootings that shock international public opinion. When the Covid-19 health crisis began to take hold in the United States, the world witnessed a veritable rush of Americans to buy guns, with sales records being broken. This context allowed us to fear the worst in an uncertain environment, which was even more so since other cases compromised social stability: the denounced police violence that led to crowd effects in the streets.

In the United States, there is a particular approach to life among certain survivalist individuals who do not hesitate to build up considerable stocks of food and weapons to resist a nuclear war or any form of catastrophe whose effects would be lasting. This is how some have built underground shelters to protect themselves for several months or years if necessary. With the advent of Covid-19 and social tensions, the sense of global fear grew to the point that Americans sought to protect themselves by any means necessary. The sale of arms and ammunition has exploded, more so in a poisonous national political context where a split is now observable between those who defend Joe Biden's victory and those who consider the election to have been rigged, thus raising fears of a risk of overflow. The NRA is systematically singled out when a tragic event occurs, and an individual perpetrates a dastardly act with firearms. However, despite the criticism, the NRA is serene because its power of influence is considerable. To campaign against this association is to alienate a powerful electoral vector that will focus its attention on politicians who defend the right to arm themselves freely.

It is in a similar electoral logic that we must consider the energy lobbies and in particular the powerful oil lobby. The energy sector represents ten million jobs in the United States. An economic crisis is potentially destructive for this strategic sector of activity for the national economy but also for any politician wishing to be re-elected. Not having the support of the oil lobby is a handicap. Losing it is probably worse. Any energy crisis is a disaster for any political leader because the consequences are quick and violent. This is what happened in April 2020 with the abysmal fall in WTI trading prices to negative levels. Although Donald Trump's reaction was immediate, great damage had already been done to the oil industry, which had been prospering since the Obama Administration's decision to focus on a policy of intensive production of shale oil and gas. This new production activity was a blessing for many producers as well as for the national economy. The United States became the world's largest oil producer, and with the volumes produced, dependence on imports was reduced and the country began to export its hydrocarbons. Despite the restrictions promoted by the Obama Administration to preserve certain regions and to assert himself as an actor committed to fighting global warming, Donald Trump saw the oil sector as a sort of golden goose that needed to be protected and satisfied. Declaring himself a climate skeptic, he took the opposite view of the environmental policies decided by his predecessor to grant oil producers optimal business conditions: increase production while influencing the available supply and consequently playing on the exchange prices. Donald Trump's objective was clear: to favor American producers on international markets and to ensure that Americans have access to low-cost oil products. His goals were achieved. Shale oil and gas have reshuffled the deck in the oil and gas market: the United States is full of them, exploiting them at maximum efficiency while enjoying favorable economic conditions, since shale oil is quick to develop and much less expensive than traditional oil. The plan worked perfectly, especially since international competitors were having difficulty agreeing on a production policy that would be revised downwards to halt the negative trend in exchange prices. The conditions were thus very favorable to American producers, who amassed considerable profits. The system reached its limits with Covid-19, the fall in world demand and a supply that had not adapted to the reality of the situation. Prices collapsed and the oil industry was suddenly in chaos, weakened and unprepared to face such an unfavorable whirlwind. Within a few weeks, many producers had to resign themselves to ceasing their activity.

Sectoral support and Donald Trump's vain obstinacy
This combination of circumstances worked against Donald Trump. While he had exceptional popularity ratings for a three-year incumbent and the November 2020 presidential election looked like a formality, he was shaken by a situation that began to spin out of control. As Covid-19 began to claim its first victims, he was widely criticized for crisis management that was not well perceived by the electorate. As mentioned above, in addition to this unprecedented health context, social tensions were rekindled against a backdrop of police violence and racial tensions due to several tragic cases that mobilized the population in several large cities of the country. Finally, the economic catastrophe caused by the health crisis left tens of millions of people in a very precarious personal situation due to the numerous job cuts. There was a rebound in the U.S. economy that allowed for the creation of new jobs, but

the jobs crisis was not over. It was under these circumstances that Biden began to emerge as a potential presidential candidate. As time went on, pollsters gave the former U.S. Vice-President increasing numbers of votes, until the breaking point when he really began to soar in the polls. This trend was reduced, however, as the presidential election approached, even though he had a comfortable lead according to the pollsters.

But Donald Trump was determined to turn the tide and fight a ruthless battle that he was sure would be won - unless, he said, the election was rigged. Joe Biden ran a calm campaign, wanting to show that he could respond with authority to his opponent's attacks. In addition, the specter of 2016 reappeared, as doubts had been raised about the reliability of the methodology of the American polling institutes, which, it must be admitted, had misjudged the situation. Of course, the result proved them right for 2020. Joe Biden undoubtedly won the election, but the fight was much closer than predicted.

On November 3, the predicted trend began to take shape. The Democrats had the upper hand in the House of Representatives. As for the Senate, the duel between the two major parties promised to be intense, with no clear majority emerging. As for the battle for the White House, they quickly gave the Democratic candidate an advantage. It was in this stormy context that tradition was broken, and Donald Trump refused to concede defeat, preferring to carry out what he had announced beforehand and to contest the validity of the election. In his eyes, there was no doubt that an adverse victory could only have been conditioned by fraud. Thus, he undertook the filing of numerous legal actions to bring proof of irregularities in the organization of the vote.

More than two weeks after the big election day, he has not been able to provide evidence to validate his suspicions. He must now face the facts and accept defeat, something he is not used to doing. However, he will have no choice but to leave the White House on January 20. Joe Biden will then officially become the 46th President in the history of the United States of America. A period of two months traditionally allows for a gradual political transition. The latter is considerably disrupted by the unwillingness of Donald Trump to obstruct the democratic functioning of the institutions. Any argument that could harm the future Biden presidency can be the subject of decisions aimed at making his task even more difficult. One of them is to confront him with a contradiction: the man who has pledged to implement energy policies to reduce the influence of oil will have a hard time putting his plan into action. Donald Trump is working on this.

Similarly, the economic and geopolitical context is not conducive to a future US disengagement from the oil sector. It is more likely that Joe Biden will be forced to maintain a course of high production of oil and shale gas in order not to penalize a sector of activity that provides many jobs, but which also contributes to maintaining the influence of the United States on the world political scene. Therefore, Donald Trump made it sound as if he was not opposed to a military strike in Iran before January 20... This announcement will probably not be followed up, but it has obviously provoked the wrath of the Iranian leaders who are promising terrible reprisals if such a scenario were to occur. The aim of the maneuver was rather to provoke the future Biden Administration and to embarrass it by having to deal with an Iranian problem which, however, is likely to displease the Arab allies of the Persian Gulf. Clearly, if Joe Biden agrees to deal with Iran as Barack Obama did in his time, important consequences will be expected on the oil markets, especially if a relaxation of sanctions against Tehran were to be considered. If Iran is allowed to export again on the international market, trading prices will be fatally affected unless other producers agree to reduce their production, which is unlikely given that all of them are in dire need of clearing stocks and generating revenues.

A change of direction in governance to come

Three weeks after the presidential election, Donald Trump finally seems ready to accept the principle of transition, even if he persists in refusing any form of electoral defeat while the legal appeals filed come back against him. Meanwhile, Joe Biden has been working on the outline of his next Administration and a first draft shows several names of future heads of Administration. Antony Blinken's name was put forward as Secretary of State to succeed Mike Pompeo. If Susan Rice's name had seemed for a few days to be the favorite for American diplomacy, it is finally a man who is a fervent defender of multilateralism who will lead the national foreign policy. It is the confirmation that a new diplomatic course will be deployed and that it will take the opposite direction of what was undertaken by Donald Trump. It is also the confirmation that the United States will quickly tackle issues dear to Joe Biden and which marked the Trump diplomacy: the withdrawal from the Paris Climate Agreement as well as the withdrawal from the Iranian nuclear agreement. Logic dictates that he will put in place the necessary mechanisms that will undo what Donald Trump had decided and which went against the public policies developed by Barack Obama. Thus, a gesture of openness towards Iran will necessarily be an act whose scope will go far beyond the symbolic framework. He will have to show a formidable capacity for diplomacy in order not to upset the Middle Eastern allies that Donald Trump has ended up "retaining" by bringing the State of Israel closer to several Arab hydrocarbon-producing monarchies. The initiative of the 45th President of the United States was a maneuver aimed at ensuring the continuity of his diplomatic action in case of re-election or a desire to upset or complicate the task of his successor in case of defeat. Several readings are possible, even if the lexical field of defeat is strongly disapproved within the Trump clan. Perhaps he managed to seal this diplomatic agreement because the voting trends were unfavorable to him at the time, and he was secretly contemplating the specter of an electoral defeat... Perhaps one day soon he will deliver his impressions and feelings in his future memoirs.

In the meantime, the Middle East is apprehensive about Joe Biden's first steps and decisions. A reopening of the dialogue with Tehran is likely to weaken everything that has been undertaken with Saudi Arabia and Israel in particular, who will see in any gesture of openness to discussion a reason to distance themselves from the United States and to move closer to Russia. This is just one example, but this region, which is subject to so many long-lasting tensions, is not only the object of local or even regional tensions or conflicts. Indeed, there is a power struggle at an external level between several major international political powers, including the United States and Russia. In short, a gesture of openness towards the Islamic Republic of Iran is likely to generate major consequences on the oil markets in the short or medium term, including the hypothesis of an increase in the global supply of black gold on the international markets if some of the sanctions on Iranian oil exports were to be lifted. Such a scenario would be an economic disaster for the major international producers, but it could also satisfy the interests of American oil companies if trading prices were to "stabilize" at a low level, i.e., insufficient to ensure a balanced budget for Saudi Arabia and Russia, but sufficient to allow American companies to generate profits. This scenario is hypothetical. There are others.

Our point is this: while nothing is impossible in international relations, it will be very difficult for the new American diplomacy to engage in a new dialogue with Iran without upsetting Saudi Arabia, its Arab allies, and the State of Israel. The Biden Administration will have to be firm with Tehran. It will probably be less perilous to reinstate the Paris Climate Agreement, an upcoming act that will receive international praise. However, it will be up to the new President-elect to put in place a coherent energy program that improves on what he opposes his predecessor on climate issues. We should not only hope for symbolic gestures or initiatives, but also for concrete actions and results. But our reasoning leads us to believe that American oil still has a bright future ahead, that the American oil sector should continue to operate at full capacity. Perhaps under Biden's watch the US will succeed in reducing its consumption of greenhouse gas emitting energy. However, if the domestic oil industry continues to produce, it means that whatever is saved in the US will be consumed elsewhere, and that may not lead to any improvement in the fight against global warming. We are beginning to discern the future outlines of American diplomacy. They are commendable in our eyes, but they will come up against the disapproval of states that were close to the White House under the Trump Administration. Diplomacy is the work of men and women. International relations are subject to evolving alliance games. We are at the dawn of a new era that will bring its share of joys and sorrows.

Openness and diplomatic pragmatism in sight
In the world of international relations, the rules of the game are well known. In the United States, everyone knows that an Administration lasts a minimum of four years

or a maximum of eight years when the President-elect completes his full term. Because of the political alternation, everyone also knows that a newly elected President will have a different foreign policy vision than his predecessor. It can happen that a head of state changes his vision during his term. Let us remember the example of George W. Bush, whose first term was very much influenced by the events of September 11, 2001, a term in which the neo-conservative influence was omnipresent, and which militated for an interventionist but above all unilateralist vision. The second presidential term of the 43rd President of the United States differed since the national foreign policy was then less interventionist and placed under the seal of dialogue. His successor advocated the gradual withdrawal of American troops from Iraq and Afghanistan. Similarly, he promoted a less rigorous diplomacy towards Iran, a country that had previously been named as part of the *Axis of Evil* by George W. Bush. Each newly elected President in the United States dictates his diplomacy and consequently surrounds himself with a Secretary of State who will act in the direction of his foreign policy vision.

With the next Biden term, the new Administration is taking shape and foreign policy is likely to move towards a new dialogue with the international community, bringing a new breath of fresh air that may reassure some and terrify others. The example of the Middle East is illustrative of this situation, since Tehran's desire to advocate a more dialogue-oriented diplomacy with Iran may be seen as a positive sign that will not be perceived in the same way by Riyadh and Jerusalem. Similarly, what will be the American position towards North Korea? Everyone remembers the surprising about-face of Donald Trump who accepted the principle of meeting Kim Jong-Un and making him a "friend", a personal relationship that went as far as a symbolic search of North Korean territory near the demilitarized zone separating the two Koreas, while the latter had begun his term of office with a very firm position towards Pyongyang... and which could augur the worst with a potential fear of triggering an armed conflict. Donald Trump had taken his Administration and his Secretary of State by surprise when he undertook to contact the North Korean leader, sure of his strength and his ability to impose his wishes on him in terms of denuclearization. It was a resounding failure, never admitted as such by the New York real estate tycoon, but North Korea never gave in to the White House's demands. Since then, Washington-Pyongyang relations have been on standby. It seems unlikely, however, that the new Biden Administration will go down a path like the one undertaken by Donald Trump. Joe Biden will not risk an affront by engaging in "soft" diplomacy for an expected result that he will not achieve. Donald Trump has been wrong on the North Korean case. He has underestimated the reality of the situation and especially the weight of Chinese influence in the decisions taken by Kim Jong-Un.

China is among the great challenges ahead for American diplomacy. Joe Biden has made it clear that he wants to maintain American greatness and not alienate its political and economic leadership. This sends a message to China and other foreign powers that openness to dialogue should not be equated with American weakness. In this sense, the North Korean issue cannot be managed as it was by Donald Trump. It constitutes a political and diplomatic argument in the context of the rivalry between China and the United States. Similarly, the new President Biden was criticized by his predecessor for his personal relations with Chinese dignitaries and businessmen. He will therefore have to show that the United States does not intend to do anything that could be perceived by the American public as a form of acknowledged weakness towards China. The

North Korean example is very revealing of the fact that American diplomacy is going to evolve considerably over the next four years.

All of this leads us to believe that the task to be assumed in terms of energy policy, as promised during the election campaign, will be more complicated than it seems because the diplomatic problems will be numerous and will constitute difficulties to be overcome or surpassed to effectively promote this plan to fight global warming, which must necessarily involve a future reduction in the consumption of hydrocarbons. In other words, the whole question rests on the Cornelian choice of putting in place a policy of means or of providing the means for its policy. Joe Biden will have to quickly impose his style from the moment he is inaugurated. There is no doubt that he intends to make a firm commitment to the fight against global warming and that he will opt for the reintegration of the United States into the Paris Climate Agreement as soon as possible. This does not necessarily imply that he will engage in a policy of reducing oil dependence. However, he will undoubtedly pursue the policy of new energies, including hydrogen, an option already highlighted under the Trump presidency but for which there has been, curiously, too little communication.

Conclusion

The major diplomatic and strategic issues at stake may indeed thwart the laudable intentions of the new American President, who will quickly want to rejoin the Paris Agreement to reassure the international community. However, even if he has already mentioned his economic plans, which are close to those once promoted by Barack Obama, the price of oil products will be a major issue in American public opinion in view of the mid-term elections in November 2022. Already marked by a severe economic crisis due to Covid-19, public opinion will be sensitive to concrete achievements and especially what constitutes necessary spending in American households. Everyone knows that Americans are heavy consumers of petroleum products, the heaviest consumers in the world. This is in a sense what drives the desire to address the nation's dependence on oil while Donald Trump was able to allow reasonable access prices for the American consumer. If Joe Biden wants to stay the course, he will have to juggle skillfully and find the right balance. If his wish is to keep his fellow citizens satisfied with low-priced petroleum products, this will only be possible by maintaining high levels of black gold production and encouraging the development of shale oil. This is the most logical consequence. However, there is no indication that this is the option that will be chosen. If this hypothesis were to be validated, the oil lobby would have good reason to rejoice.

Similarly, international issues tend to play in favor of this thinking because the best way to weaken the other major oil powers is to maintain a production policy that manages to keep exchange prices relatively low. This amounts to playing on the available supply. This hypothesis is even more conceivable if the new American diplomacy were to attract the wrath of Saudi Arabia. A reopening of discussions with Iran will be badly perceived in the Wahhabi kingdom. We remember the official visit of Barack Obama who came to announce his intention to ease tensions with Iran over the nuclear issue. This was perceived as a betrayal in Riyadh. Joe Biden is thus taking the risk of exposing himself to a similar reaction. But the Saudi Achilles' heel is precisely oil. The national economy of this Arab country relies almost exclusively on the sale of oil. The current situation is largely unfavorable to the Wahhabi kingdom because the exchange prices are far below the levels that would allow the country to re-establish a budget balance, while Saudi society is very dependent on the activity of Saudi Aramco. The Saudi weakness is its dependence on oil revenues. The lack of sectoral diversity and the fact that most jobs are financed directly or indirectly by Saudi Aramco puts Riyadh in a very uncomfortable position if the US were to maintain caps on black gold production aimed at unbalancing the supply-demand ratio in favor of supply. The repercussions are potentially catastrophic for Saudi Arabia. The United States thus has a means of pressure. However, will it seek to make susceptible allies who have strengthened their ties with the United States under Donald Trump? Similarly, is there not a risk of compromising the diplomatic advances negotiated and endorsed by several Arab states and the State of Israel? These are two questions among others that raise the possible consequences of a reopening of dialogue with Iran.

In absolute terms, the best American diplomatic weapon to date is its influence on the world oil market. It is in this sense that black gold remains the natural resource with the greatest strategic power. If Saudi Arabia had a domestic economy that was much less dependent on oil, it would likely have more room to maneuver without risking its economic balance. This leads us to believe that an American gesture towards Iran will not be well received in Riyadh, but that the Wahhabi kingdom will not be able to afford to be too vehement, because Joe Biden will have the trump card: the power to influence market prices. Everything is negotiated, willy-nilly. Everything is reversible, evolving, or modifiable if the actors involved agree on a common policy that, while not satisfying everyone, allows everyone to find an interest. Joe Biden's first steps as President of the United States will be scrutinized by the entire international community. He will be awaited at the turn. If his intention is to maintain an unwavering American position in international competition, he will have to make decisions that depart from what were campaign promises. In such a perspective, it will be difficult for him to win diplomatic victories without relying on the American oil sector, which constitutes a major asset for the defense of strategic interests on the international scene. Nothing is obviously set in stone, and it is quite possible that the new Administration will opt for a different strategy compatible with a decline in American oil activity. However, the arguments put forward will have to be extremely persuasive.

Joe Biden's big challenge
January 2021

On Wednesday, January 20, 2021, in front of the Capitol, a symbolic place of American democracy, Joe Biden will be sworn in as the 46th President in the history of the United States of America. The images of the ceremony will be relayed by the world's media. It will be a form of finalization or consecration for the man who won the presidential election a few weeks earlier and who then faced Donald Trump's categorical refusal to acknowledge any defeat without referring to alleged electoral fraud. In December, the Unites States Electoral College officially recognized the victory of the Democratic candidate, a decision that was in turn definitively acted upon by Congress... while outside, in the streets of Washington, the incumbent President spoke before a large and supportive audience that, like his champion, refused to recognize Joe Biden's election victory. Once the speech was over, a scene took place that was unimaginable in the United States: the invasion of the Capitol by demonstrators who wanted to contest the legitimacy of the Democratic victory, while Congress was meeting at that very moment to act on it. The members of Congress had to be evacuated in a hurry to a safe place. The rest was a succession of shocking images. The invasion of the Capitol was the culmination of a global malaise that has plagued the United States for several years, perhaps since Donald Trump took office in 2017. It is difficult to date a starting point for what has become evident over time: American society is deeply divided.

Short of delivering a speculative thesis on why Capitol Hill was invaded, it is important to understand that Donald Trump has retained strong popular support despite everything. He is probably the most popular President in national history. At the risk of being wrong in our analysis, he had the cards in his hand to win the presidential election. He played them badly. He lost not because Joe Biden was more popular than he was, but because he probably disappointed or annoyed too many people who ultimately decided to vote for the Democratic candidate… and to vote against Donald Trump. The latter could boast a very flattering record at the end of 2019. He then enjoyed an exceptional popularity rating after three years in the White House.

At the beginning of 2020, when the Democratic primaries were revealing candidates with strong presidential ambitions and Joe Biden was in trouble before taking a decisive lead on Super Tuesday, the Democratic chances for a final victory seemed slim because no one saw what could prevent the eccentric and whimsical Donald Trump from winning a second presidential term. There was, however, one disruptive element that was not well appreciated by the strongman in the White House: The Covid-19 pandemic. This pandemic spread across the Northern hemisphere at a rapid pace, becoming a major health problem in a matter of weeks. In the United States, the first reported cases were quickly followed on the East Coast by the first deaths. Images of New York hospitals overwhelmed by the influx of new patients, the distress of medical staff and the unbearable images of dead bodies piled on top of each other to show the rapid and frightening increase in the number of deaths attributed to Covid-19 were widely reported in the United States and around the world. Donald Trump was asked to act, to make decisions to try to stop the devastating effects of the pandemic as soon as possible, both for the national population and for the economic system. From a few dozen, the victims quickly became hundreds, then thousands, then tens of thousands. This form of coronavirus then migrated to the Southern states but also to the West. During this time, Donald Trump gave the impression of minimizing the effects of Covid-19 and made several communications on the subject that shocked public opinion. People were dying and the national economy was simultaneously shaken by the health crisis. Between the deaths and the many job losses, Donald Trump clearly did not satisfy most of the population. His popularity rating declined. Voting intentions for the future Democratic candidate began to take off, to the point that pollsters made Joe Biden, who had finally won the Democratic nomination, the favorite in the election.

Meanwhile, rather than understanding the popular disapproval of him, Donald Trump continued to communicate as he always has. Between provocations, clumsiness, and other names whose purpose is to show everything that could play in his disadvantage, the 45th President of the United States has put himself at the back of many people ... while he still retained an important base of support. This is probably what gave him the illusion that nothing could happen to him and that he could only win the election on November 3, 2020. In the meantime, the health situation in the United States continued to worsen by the day and an old demon began to resurface with social tensions. Several high-profile cases of police interventions with dramatic outcomes led black populations to denounce cases of police mistreatment of people of color that were too frequent and above all unjustified. Large-scale movements took shape in several American metropolises, but Donald Trump did not give the impression that he wanted to calm social tensions. Here again, several statements made by him, intentional or clumsy, shocked people. Everything that could be forgiven between 2017 and 2019 was no longer forgiven in 2020. The health and economic crisis and then racial tensions were too thorny. Their crisis management was poor. As for communication, it did not live up to the electorate's expectations. The November 3 vote sanctioned all this.

Donald Trump was fueled by an unshakeable faith in his chances of electoral success, convinced that he was loved enough to win his second presidential bet after 2016. He undoubtedly lacked discernment, misjudged the reality of things, and his true popularity and especially the burgeoning, growing unpopularity that would eventually become an insurmountable divide. He always claimed that the word "defeat" was not in his vocabulary. Yet, months before the election, he had begun to spread the message that a Democratic victory could only come from voter fraud and that he would work to avoid admitting defeat if it did, as if he sensed that the specter of defeat remained a possibility. This communication was already dangerous because it implied that the electoral system was biased in favor of the Democrats. In short, he had announced in advance what he would do, except that the November 3 verdict was probably a cold shower for him, so convinced of his strength and his ability to overcome any obstacle that stood in his way. He refused to admit defeat. His speech sounded like a threat to American democracy. He was convinced that he had been the victim of a rigged election, and he wanted to have this recognized by the courts, which saw the emergence of numerous actions in which no request led to a conclusion in the direction of anomalies found in the votes. Despite this, he persisted in denying defeat, promising to do everything he could to undermine the transition of power. This he did. Everything was set in motion to disrupt the transition of power, with bad faith and a dangerous rhetoric of electoral fraud being maintained, which influenced his most ardent supporters, some of whom were convinced by the thesis of a large-scale fraud.

In December 2020, several members of Donald Trump's inner circle, some of whom had probably realized that no electoral fraud would be proven, and others who were rather weary of Donald Trump's polemical communication, submitted their resignations. These people probably wanted to show their boss that his actions were not conducive to appeasing the situation. His behavior and communication represented a risk for the future of democracy in the United States. However, he kept some support among the elected Republicans, but when Congress met to definitively validate Joe Biden's electoral victory, and faced with the invasion of the Capitol, which shook all the national institutions that guarantee democracy, some elected Republicans officially recognized the victory of the Democratic candidate, thus signifying to Donald Trump the end of the game, making him understand that anything that aimed to hinder the process of transfer of power would no longer be supported by the conservative party. Donald Trump's overall attitude was very damaging for the whole of the United States. The country was on the verge of chaos, and it was important to find the right solutions to bring social peace as soon as possible. American society is deeply divided. Joe Biden knows this. As for the institutions that guarantee the democratic spirit in the United States, they now fear for the security of the person who will be sworn in on January 20.

After the events of January 6, any scenario is unfortunately possible. That is why the number of National Guard personnel mobilized to secure the city of Washington is unprecedented. Several days before the swearing-in, the whole world could discover an American capital that had taken on the appearance of a city under siege, seemingly depopulated of its ordinary population and giving the impression of being occupied only by police and military forces. The swearing-in ceremony took place in a strange atmosphere. It was going to be special because of the health protocols that had to be considered with respect to Covid-19. It was also going to be more so because of the absence of Donald Trump who will have been able to show until the end a face of bad loser which will not plead in his favor. Traditionally, the outgoing President attends the inauguration ceremony of the newly elected President. This symbolic presence is not mandatory. Its purpose is to convey the message that democracy is the most important thing in the United States. A political transition takes place in the context of a victory of the opposing camp and constitutes an official recognition that it is the people's choice that has been expressed. Donald Trump will certainly leave a negative image because of all that was undertaken at the end of his reign to contest and fiercely deny his defeat, at the risk of unleashing passions and putting his country in jeopardy because of motivations for which the federal and state justice system has never recognized anything that goes in the direction of fraud in the organization and conduct of the vote for the presidential election. To the end, Donald Trump will have denied the evidence. Until the end, he will have used all the stratagems to make it more difficult for his successor to take office. For the latter, it will be imperative to take control of operations and find the right words to reassure the national population to heal its ills that have seemed so exacerbated in 2020.

Two main priorities

Once he is sworn in, he will be officially inaugurated as the 46th President of the United States. The whole thing will take place in a unique and unprecedented atmosphere. The streets around the Capitol will be almost deserted, mainly occupied by the National Guard forces deployed in large numbers for the occasion. Indeed, the occurrence of an attack against the person of the new President would be the worst thing that could happen in the

United States while the social climate is particularly disturbed. Indeed, the authorities fear that there will be outbursts in the days following the inauguration ceremony. They would come from the most fervent pro-Trump supporters and could occur in any American community. There are still many people who remain convinced that the presidential election was rigged and that therefore Joe Biden has no legitimacy to lead the United States of America. The social climate is indeed very sensitive. The presidential election has clearly exacerbated tensions, which have snowballed into several cumulative factors, though not exhaustive, that have contributed to an ever-deepening division among the national population. Before the Covid-19, it would not be fair to say that all was well in the United States. Rather, consider the image of the tree that hid the forest. Donald Trump was hiding behind a flattering economic record, but within the American population, the damage was already deep.

For many years, African-Americans had been speaking out against injustices committed by police forces, particularly by white officers. When the pandemic crisis caught up with Uncle Sam's country, things took a new turn. The economic downturn had many negative consequences for many Americans, with job losses numbering in the tens of millions nationwide. In addition, there is the health issue that has been so divisive and debatable. Donald Trump has underestimated the gravity of the situation. He has never been able to find the right words to explain that this form of coronavirus can occur in different ways and that it will not impact infected individuals in the same way. The mortality rate is relatively low compared to the number of infected individuals. This does not mean, however, that the level of severity should be underestimated. The power of image is considerable. Americans, for some, were shocked by Donald Trump's statements and communications when the media relayed reports of overcrowded hospitals, lack of logistics, and cases of individuals who could not be placed in resuscitation units because medical authorities were so unprepared for such a wave. As mentioned in the introductory section, one is reminded of the shocking images of mass graves that were hastily dug up in New York State at the height of the epidemic, when the dead were pouring in at such a high rate that funeral homes were unable to handle all the "clients". Donald Trump clearly mishandled the health crisis. It did him a great disservice to his election campaign when, in January 2020, the polls showed him as the clear winner on November 3, no matter which Democratic candidate he faced. He was certainly known for his explosive, boiling, unrestrained and very raw communication. That is why he left no one indifferent. His supporters, though numerous, were ready to accept anything from him, even the most fanciful ideas. Many were also seduced for a while by his speech, undoubtedly delighted by the country's economic performance, but who withdrew over time at the mercy of the sulphureous communications of which he was a master in the matter. This was not to be the case with the Covid-19 pandemic crisis.

As Joe Biden prepares to take over the political and economic governance of the country, nearly four hundred thousand deaths have been officially attributed to the coronavirus in one year across the country. This is considerable. On the other hand, the sanitary situation still seems to be out of control. California is currently experiencing the ravages of Covid-19, with its Governor having decided to confine the most populous state in the federation. It is unfortunately to be expected that the statistical lines will soon see the human toll increase, while the President-elect, before being officially inaugurated, had made a communication operation by being publicly vaccinated. The health crisis is serious. The social crisis is just as serious. Donald Trump is leaving the White House while the country continues to live through painful hours where social peace has become an issue of absolute urgency. Indeed, tensions are high, and while it is to be hoped that things will gradually return to normal over time, that the discontent of Donald Trump's supporters will subside, or that the media will be less concerned with other priorities defined by the new Biden Administration, the risk of social disorder exists. For this reason, it is incumbent upon Joe Biden to quickly find the words that will ease tensions, to set himself up as a champion of peace, to promote a discourse of equality in a country where communities feel so much injustice in relation to what is done in other countries. A huge communication task awaits the newly elected President.

Highly anticipated on the international scene
It is easy to criticize a choice or a decision. Once he won the Democratic nomination to challenge Donald Trump, his speech was generally sober, more measured than that of his opponent. He didn't send his fellow citizens into a trance-like state with promises that were each more incredible than the last. No. He did not over-promise. He acted as a reasonable and rational politician. His overall plan was in line with what had been undertaken by the man he once served for eight years, Barack Obama. He put forward a social dimension that Donald Trump rejected. In short, the confrontation was logical. Donald Trump meticulously unraveled everything he could that was put in place by Barack Obama, both in domestic and foreign policy. Joe Biden will do the same with what was put in place by Donald Trump, considering that he now has a congressional Democratic majority in both Houses. Joe Biden intends to put in place a health care system that was promoted by Barack Obama in his time.

On the international scene, he also intends to make a radical shift by repositioning the United States on the world stage as a state with which dialogue is possible. Dialogue and openness are thus the key words of the diplomacy that the new Administration intends to put in place. This was already stated by Joe Biden during his election campaign. This is how he declared that he wanted to reopen discussions with Iran. In intention, the Iranian example is striking for American voters. This *rogue state*, reviled during the Trump era, is once again an actor in international relations with whom it is possible to discuss and with whom dialogue is necessary. In short, the idea was to show the American people that diplomatic crises can be resolved through dialogue without necessarily triggering an armed conflict. The intention was good but misguided.

Indeed, Joe Biden got himself into trouble by proclaiming his intention to renew a dialogue with Tehran. This was tantamount to overshadowing the diplomatic agreement sealed a few weeks earlier between several Middle Eastern Arab countries and the State of Israel. This was Donald Trump's latest stunt on the international scene: bringing together at a table state leaders who are nevertheless opposed to each other. Yes, but the Arab oil-monarchies and Israel have a common enemy: Iran. During his election campaign, Joe Biden undoubtedly made a mistake by stating his intentions towards Iran. He thus raised doubts in Jerusalem, Riyadh and some other capitals that hate Tehran. In short, he got himself into trouble. He was under no obligation to mention the Iranian case explicitly. He could invoke the desire to assert the spirit of diplomacy in his foreign policy rather than favor the threat of the use of armed force. This stance on the Iranian nuclear issue has created a climate of mistrust in the Middle East towards Washington.

Without mentioning any causal link, China then put serious pressure on Joe Biden. Beijing's official line is very clear. Despite the Biden family's long-standing relationship with China, personal friendships will not take precedence over state interests. Xi Jinping and Donald Trump had engaged in a merciless duel. It was to the one who would penalize the most the economic interests of his adversary, without counting the technological rivalry for which China knew how to show that it was now capable of competing or even surpassing its American competitor. The Huawei affair is not just a case of alleged espionage. The 5G technology that Huawei had the ambition to spread around the world struck the American minds that their Chinese competitors could design very high-performance technologies. On the other hand, China continues to promote ambitious space programs and does not despair of sending a manned mission to the Moon in the current decade. Several technological missions to the Moon and Mars have shown that China has know-how that is second to none. It is a way to show muscle, as in the Cold War, when the stakes of space conquest were part of the communication plans to impress the opposing camp, to show an economic strength that could promote these programs, the power of scientific advances and, of course, the control of the atom.

Joe Biden should expect no favors from China. He will immediately be put to the test by Beijing, which will try to understand what kind of President he will be. He will hardly have had time to be inaugurated in the White House before he will have to tackle burning issues, both in domestic and foreign policy. It will be up to him to set the right pace, to be accepted by everyone, to be recognized as a great statesman who is unanimously respected. The first few weeks of governance will be crucial for the rest of his presidential term, and he knows it. Let's remember that the end of Obama's reign was marked by fresh relations with

Israel, Saudi Arabia, China, but also Russia, which nobody is talking about in Washington now...

An inauguration marked by a speech on national unity and a return to peaceful relations with the West

It was the long-awaited moment of Joe Biden's inauguration day: the first speech of the new President in office. Not surprisingly, the message hammered home was one of national unity and appeasement. It was the right direction to take. It was imperative. He had to set the pace immediately, to show himself to be a unifying force and to bring people together. The content of the speech is good. It was necessary to reassure, to calm and above all to show a sign of openness with the adversity that refuses the democratic victory. It is desirable that the speech was well heard and perceived, that tensions fade and that the fight against the Covid-19 pandemic quickly becomes the major concern of the new Administration. The public must be reassured. This is what the American people needed to hear. No one knows what will happen to what appears to be a social divide in the United States, but Joe Biden's first presidential speech was well-intentioned. He cannot be blamed for not addressing the social ills of his country, which in the final weeks of the Trump presidency have severely threatened the democratic sustainability of institutions. The most difficult task awaits the newly inaugurated President: to get his peacemaking message across, to make sure that it is heard and convincing, so that the most recalcitrant will in turn be persuaded to put aside their protesting tendencies for the sake of democratic continuity. An internal malaise can only be detrimental to the United States on the international scene, whose credibility was strongly affected by the events of January 6, 2021, with the invasion of the Capitol, which shocked the international community.

He promised to get to work on his first day as president. He signed many executive orders. He said he wanted to put forward his ideas and put an end to decisions made by Donald Trump that he did not agree with. Thus, one of his priorities was to get the United States back into the Paris Climate Agreement. He intends to restore a new image of the United States in the world, especially with traditional Western allies who had distanced themselves from Washington during the Trump era. It is important for him to restore courteous, friendly and above all collegial relations with the West. He is described as a friend of Europe. The decision to engage the services of Antony Blinken is consistent with the aim of re-establishing complicit relations with Europe, but also with Canada, a country led by Justin Trudeau, who had little taste for Trump's methods. It is now time for the United States to make a new diplomatic turn and return to an approach to international relations placed under the seal of collegiality with old allies, in short to restore the NATO spirit that had suffered so much under the American presidency of Donald Trump. The stakes will be all the higher for the United States because, as indicated in the previous section, the new master of the White House will be expected to take a hard look at many international problems.

In the Middle East, he has been viewed with suspicion since he expressed his desire to tackle the Iranian nuclear issue in a more flexible management climate than that established by his predecessor. China will also test Joe Biden's resistance, to understand what kind of statesman he will be on the international scene, knowing that the latter understands he will have to deal with Chinese ambitions which are no longer hidden: China intends to dethrone the United States from their global economic leadership. As for Russia, a subtle message was addressed to the new American President, suggesting that it was up to the United

States to determine the direction that would be given to Moscow-Washington relations, a way to put pressure on Joe Biden and Antony Blinken. Russia is aware that the United States intends to reactivate its good diplomatic relations with Europe, which in absolute terms does not argue for a warming of relations between the White House and the Kremlin.

Russia is among the countries that have sent an undisguised message to Joe Biden. It has no interest now in manifesting itself as a country wishing to impose pressure. It is better for it to keep a low profile and observe what others are doing before acting. President Putin is a fine strategist. He is aware of his strengths but also knows that his country does not have the same means of pressure as its Chinese neighbor. He is therefore in the position of an observer, knowing moreover that his country is in the crosshairs of the American Democratic leaders who still show as much reluctance towards Russia. It is now up to Joe Biden to decide on the direction he intends to take with Moscow, knowing that he will already have to prove himself on the Iranian issue and in his competitive relations with China.

Sudden change of tone in the Chinese speech
The day after Joe Biden's inauguration, Beijing's communication suddenly changed. The Chinese capital had shown itself to be offensive and almost threatening towards the new strongman of the United States. The idea was undoubtedly to intimidate him and to display its uncompromising ambitions of fierce competition, the goal of which is to become the number one in the world economy. Joe Biden made it clear that he would not be intimidated in this way and would do his utmost to defend his country's interests, not accepting anything imposed from China. Although it is known that the Biden family and the

Middle Kingdom have long had friendly ties, the former Senator from Delaware and Vice-President under Barack Obama is aware of the leadership stakes that are being played out between his country and its main rival. Donald Trump has made this competition a battle horse, one that led to complicated diplomatic relations between Washington and Beijing... As for trade relations, it was up to the one who would strike a blow at the other to weaken it permanently. Donald Trump had never hidden his intention to fight with Xi Jinping, to show China that the United States did not intend to be dethroned from its seat of leadership in politics and the world economy. This is how he engaged in a high intensity arm-wrestling game with the war on imports, with the increased taxes, with the alleged espionage cases or with the mysterious origin of the Covid-19 pandemic for which both countries had blamed each other...

Joe Biden's image differs from that of his predecessor, who was known for his volcanic temperament and who cared little for protocol or the rules of propriety in force in the arcane world of political elites. Joe Biden is a much more politically savvy man. While he may not want to engage in a duel where Trump-style communication would be the order of the day for anything directed at China, Beijing's change in tone should be seen more as a strategy to be explored rather than a genuine policy of reaching out. Donald Trump and Joe Biden have different characters. Donald Trump wanted verbal confrontation, which materialized in strong, protectionist decisions. Biden's style will undoubtedly be different, but he will have to quickly impose his style and effectiveness. Beijing's ambitions remain unchanged. China intends to dominate the world economy.

It will be interesting to see how the new Administration will work on issues related to competing or rival countries. During the Trump presidency, if Russia had not become an official friend of the United States, the main national enemy had become China. It had mutated into the number one enemy of the American nation. Americans remember the Huawei affair, an affair that helped to reduce the weight of the tense relations traditionally maintained with Moscow since the Second World War, despite the Russiagate affair that animated American political life until 2019 and disrupted the presidency of Donald Trump. For the Democrats, Russia remained the sworn enemy of the United States. Worse, Donald Trump had been suspected of collusion with the enemy to defeat Hillary Clinton in 2016, although the investigation led by former FBI Director Robert Mueller could not reach the categorical conclusion confirming the hypothesis of collusion ... without however definitively exonerating the 45th President of the United States. The Democrats had attacked Donald Trump on Russia and the latter retorted by making China the embodiment of the great danger facing the United States. To each his own.

In the logic of things, if Joe Biden intends to pursue a foreign policy that would be in line with that of Barack Obama, Moscow would have every chance of once again becoming the bad pupil in the eyes of the White House and the State Department. This remains hypothetical because the real economic threat to the United States is obviously Chinese. The only country that has the economic means to rival or even disrupt US dominance is China, not Russia. However, it would not be surprising if the Washington-Moscow bilateral relationship were to become strained again.

As an experienced politician, Joe Biden will no doubt not make the mistake of letting his guard down in the face of China, which is now showing itself to be more friendly towards the United States. If the official communication is courteous and tends to display intentions that are as honorable as they are friendly, the economic reality that pits the two countries against each other must not be overlooked. Joe Biden knows that he will have to be firm with Beijing. If during his tenure it were to be shown that China has taken over the leadership of the world economy, Americans would see their strongman as the main architect of this setback against the Chinese rival and would then remember that Donald Trump had put in place a whole arsenal of decisions whose aim was precisely to disrupt Chinese economic interests, especially in the field of exports, a field that contributes so much to the national economic model. It is therefore to be expected that the American diplomatic positioning will change but that the real economic issues discussed will be in line with what was put in place by Donald Trump. Clearly, the United States and China are likely to engage in intense economic competition while giving the impression of courteous diplomatic relations.

Conclusion

It is undoubtedly courageous to take the reins of American political and economic governance in the current environment. The domestic and foreign policy challenges are great but also complex. The United States has reached a critical period in its history while its democratic foundations have been shaken by the end of Donald Trump's reign. Joe Biden will have to restore Americans' confidence in their institutions. He will have to make people accept that the November 3 election was not controversial at all, since until proven otherwise, no tangible evidence of election fraud has been exposed by the courts. It is understood that the management of the Covid-19 health crisis is another major project of the new Biden Administration. The promised vaccination campaign will initially aim to reassure the population, try to slow down the spread of the pandemic and the number of deaths. As for the national economy, it has been strongly affected and it will be up to the new Administration, with a majority in both Houses of Congress, to find solutions to stop a situation that has damaged the economic health of many American households.

In terms of foreign policy, the task will be difficult. Certainly, the prospect of a new rapprochement with traditional allies augurs a new diplomatic dynamic that is intended to be open-minded. The White House intends to renew friendly ties with those who had distanced themselves from Washington during the Trump governance. This seems inevitable insofar as the United States had become considerably isolated on the international scene for four years, while American economic leadership had never been so contested since 1945. The number one adversary is China, and although Beijing's official discourse has softened, it must be understood that the latter does not intend to relax its efforts to establish itself permanently at the top of the world economy. The economic competition between the two giants of the world economy is destined to last. It will be fierce. Both sides will work to weaken their rivals, even if the tone of the official discourse conveyed by the two countries will be more courteous than between 2017 and 2021. This should not obscure the true nature of this duel, which appears less bellicose than during the Trump years. Diplomacy does not erase the economic war that the two heavyweights of the world economy are waging. Joe Biden has certainly understood this. It is now up to him to determine how he will wage his duel with China while preserving his country's interests. He will revert to more conventional, gentlemanly diplomacy while standing firm to maintain economic leadership. This perspective is shared by the other traditional Western allies, who had nevertheless made a strategic rapprochement with Beijing when discussions with Donald Trump were difficult. However, despite these complex relations, the main Western economic engines had ended up distancing themselves from China. In the eyes of the 46th President of the United States, Uncle Sam's country and Europe must get along, renew stable, lasting, and sincere diplomatic and economic relations. There is strength in numbers in a multipolar global environment where all bets are off.

Although the exact origin of Covid-19 remains unclear, the WHO believes that new pandemics of this kind may emerge in the coming years and affect the international community. Scientists believe that many viruses have not yet been detected in animal species, but it should not be forgotten that a virus can become a formidable weapon in the field of international relations. The atom was the weapon that exacerbated tensions between the United States and the Soviet Union in the past. Nuclear power will no longer be the weapon that sets the tone for future international relations. It should not be understood that nuclear power is no longer a threat, which is precisely why Joe Biden hopes to find a diplomatic solution with Iran. The atom remains a threat, but there are other threats. Scientific knowledge can be used for obscure motives, and the hypothesis of a destructive virus being made in a laboratory is not fanciful. The great battles are no longer fought on the ground between armies. As we have seen for several years, the Sino-American rivalry is expressed on another terrain. Cyberattacks are now a weapon of choice. There are also economic weapons. As for laboratory inventions, they can appear at any time without being able to categorically define their origin.

If we are not to fall into a form of paranoia, we should rather consider that the means of pressure and intimidation evolve with the technological and scientific progress made. A cyberattack can be much more damaging for a country than a real armed conflict. Joe Biden knows all this, so he will have to quickly find the right balance to ensure, on the one hand, that he has the support of the American people to enter a new era of social peace. On the other hand, he will also have to find the right formula to preserve his country's interests while maintaining an edge over his Chinese rival. In the background, there is the concern to achieve a diplomatic balance that does not leave a permanent threat that could destabilize the international community and expose it to the risk of degeneration that could dangerously rock the boat to a point of no return.

President Biden takes on China... and Donald Trump
May 2021

How to kill two birds with one stone? This is undoubtedly the thought that drives the White House. The question could be put differently: how to turn a possible weakness into a strength? Covid-19 and China are inseparable since the Middle Kingdom is designated as the country that saw the birth of what was to become a widespread pandemic. Officially, at the end of May 2021, the World Health Organization counts three and half million deaths linked to this form of coronavirus one year and a half after its appearance. In the United States, this affair has undoubtedly cost his re-election to Donald Trump, who was very busy attributing responsibility to China while minimizing the danger of the pandemic that was ravaging his country. His crisis management was disastrous, and this is how he was sanctioned by the votes with all the post-election controversies that agitated the country until the nomination of Joe Biden. All of this would become ancient history, a painful national socio-political chapter that culminated in the astonishing events of January 6, 2021. They culminated in the storming of the Capitol by ardent supporters of Donald Trump who did not recognize his electoral defeat. The political transition took place under particularly sensitive conditions.

Similarly, the new President-elect immediately understood that great pressure would be brought to bear on him as soon as he took office, particularly in view of his family's long-standing relations with Ukraine and China. Older, not giving off the assurance of a strong, slender and in perfect health man, Joe Biden nevertheless assured that he intended to be a political leader who would defend the interests of his country with strength and conviction, that he would not offer any gifts to his rivals. In an America traumatized by the events of January 6 and already reeling from the health crisis and racially charged social tensions, President Biden did not intend to rely on a state of grace to take time to mature his thinking once he was inaugurated. He had to immediately opt for a reassuring and unifying speech to combat domestic ills, but he also had to instill messages to his main international rivals about what the United States intended to put in place. In short, he had to find the right balance, one that would allow him to establish himself as the political leader of the United States in the eyes of the national population and one that would help keep his country at the forefront of the world's political and economic powers.

Another issue remains: how to muzzle and discredit Donald Trump? The question is not insignificant since the former President retains a high popularity rating and despite his definitive exclusion from certain social networks, he is once again making his voice heard. Obviously, he has the firm intention to come back on the front of the stage for the presidential election of 2024 and continues in this sense to attack Joe Biden and his crisis management. Thus, the new President is not a strong man? Go and ask the Chinese! He, suspected of having personal sympathies for the Asian behemoth, is pounding his fist on the table, and summoned at the end of May 2021 the intelligence services of his country to provide him with a report within ninety days on the origins of the Covid-19, the thesis of a laboratory manipulation finding more and more echo in the United States. If China cheated or lied, it will have to face the consequences. This is what President Biden implies, even if the American scientific community does not really seem to defend the thesis of a laboratory accident, unlike the intelligence services. This difference of opinion is rather curious, but an article by Stephen Collinson has highlighted this dichotomy very well, as well as the other reason why the strongman of the White House has made this request: to understand whether the Trump Administration knew things and hid them, or whether it knowingly used them for political communication purposes. [7]

The Biden-Trump war is far from over. Using the intelligence services for an official request with international scope, given the sensitivity of the matter at hand, is a brilliant idea if it is motivated by the desire to harm another rival. In short, Joe Biden wants to know for sure, to be certain about China and the origins of the pandemic since it is now admitted that laboratory workers in the Wuhan region have been identified as having developed symptoms of Covid-19 as early as October 2019. On the other hand, he wishes to understand what information the Trump Administration really had and how it could have used it, including, and considering possible fake news for which the former President Trump would undoubtedly have to be held accountable before the federal justice system, a case that would certainly harm his political ambitions for 2024. In a few lines, here are the reasons why President Biden is calling on the national intelligence services to defend his country's interests: to put pressure on and arm himself. He is putting pressure on China, which, if it were to be accused even of negligence, would incur the wrath of the international community. As for Donald Trump, this report is obviously a weapon of choice to support any form of legal deviance that the former President might have engaged in... with a high probability of supporting evidence.

---

[7] Stephen Collinson, *"The Covid-19 origin story has massive political consequences"*, edition.cnn.com, May 27, 2021

The first official meeting of Presidents Biden and Putin

Putin

June 2021

Geneva, Switzerland, June 21, 2021

For the first time since his inauguration in January 2021, President Joe Biden traveled abroad. His European tour began with his first G7 meeting in the United Kingdom, followed by the NATO summit in Brussels and then a trip to Geneva to meet with his Russian counterpart Vladimir Putin. It was expected that the two men would take time to discuss many issues, some of which are at the heart of the difficult diplomatic relations between the two countries. The least we can say is that the mountain probably gave birth to a mouse. While the tone was courteous, the two men ultimately stuck to their respective positions, although they had each initially hinted at a willingness to work based on constructive dialogue. A significant diplomatic outcome could have been expected, but the result was a status quo. The United States demanded Russia to change its behavior and to become less hostile towards Washington and its allies. Moscow retorted and told Washington to mind its own business. The principle of the meeting between the two men was certainly a good idea. The problem is that this bilateral meeting came on the heels of two events in which President Biden had to expose what he perceived as threats to the world: China and Russia. In short, President Putin came to Switzerland with the label of threat attached to his back. The dialogue with his American alter ego had to be immediately placed under the seal of appeasement and conciliation. But this scenario did not occur. Perhaps it could have been different if President Biden had shown more consideration for Russia at the G7 and NATO summits... which would probably not have encouraged a rapprochement with traditional allies and the

European Union (EU) in particular. Perhaps it was the fault of the political agenda...

More pragmatically, it was good for the two men to meet and exchange views. Diplomacy is above all a dialogue. This being the case, there was not much to hope for, and even less for a great change. President Biden is continuing the diplomacy of Barack Obama, of whom he was the faithful Vice-President. The hoped-for rapprochement with the Western allies has certainly been successful. All converge towards the conception of a world where two threats seem more important than the others: Beijing and Moscow. In other words, President Putin could have been conciliatory, disregarding the comments made at the G7 and the NATO summit, and wanted to meet President Biden in a spirit of appeasement. Politically, this would have been to risk showing a sign of weakness towards the United States. As for President Biden, a proposal to ease tensions would make no sense in terms of credibility when he openly designates Russia as a threat to the Western alliance. The result of the race is implacable: it was difficult to hope for anything other than a status quo. The Geneva meeting had one merit: it allowed the two men to meet and exchange views face-to-face.

If we consider geopolitical issues, Russia and the United States have an interest in listening to each other on an actor who can embody the image of the threat: China. There is obviously no question of Washington and Moscow forming a common front against Beijing, but the idea is not incongruous given that Sino-Russian diplomatic relations are dictated by a pragmatic vision of this bilateral collaboration focused on trade and the purchase and sale of hydrocarbons. Historically, Russia and China have experienced mostly conflictual episodes, especially during the 20th century. The rapprochement between the two

Eurasian giants was mainly dictated by a common and realistic vision of international relations and strategic commercial imperatives. When tensions between Russia and the West intensified due to the war in Ukraine and the annexation of Crimea, Russia found a way to free itself from Western economic sanctions by intensifying its commercial relations with China, which was seeking to establish lasting relations with strategic partners for regular deliveries of gas and oil. On the other hand, Beijing and Moscow are not considered diplomatic allies. They trade with each other but are mutually suspicious of each other. In sum, the global geopolitical context means that a rational approach to diplomacy is oriented towards dialogue, which is an encouraging sign, even if the groundwork was already laid for the bilateral meeting in Geneva. If nothing definitive has been agreed in this sense, we understand that Washington-Moscow ties should remain distant but prudent.

International relations are evolving. We have seen this recently with the rapprochement between the United States and the EU. This was the expected trend, the one that was to be confirmed. Usually, political, diplomatic, and economic alliances are solid and stable, not to mention the collaboration within NATO. The Trump Administration has cast a pall over the nature of the relationship between the two sides of the Atlantic. In this sense, President Biden was able to use the right words to bring about this rapprochement that the traditional allies of the United States were hoping and waiting for. This first step is therefore validated and recorded, but it has consequences: it confirms the tense context of international relations regarding Russia and China, which are designated as threats to the Western alliance, two states that cooperate on operations of a strategic nature, notably energy. The observation is that of a fragmented international community, which is reminiscent of Samuel Huntington's clash of civilizations. [8] It is an observation: there are several poles of influence in the world. However, these poles are concerned by certain issues that pose a problem for some and which the others use to exert pressure. This is the case with the Iranian nuclear issue. It is likely that the forthcoming return of the United States to the multiparty talks will lead to a global agreement, for which the diplomatic aura would be great, and which would also have the consequence of giving Iran an image of a respectable country in the eyes of Washington, but that the negotiations could drag on because of the points of disagreement that could oppose Russians, Chinese and Western partners.

Common sense or realism should not obscure the fact that nothing is free in international relations. Everything must be paid for. There are no favors. Every agreement or concession is in fact accompanied by benefit or debt. In sum, if China and Russia manage to reach agreement with the other parties present at the talks on the Iranian nuclear case, it is likely that both will defend a much firmer position on other issues, because the principle of a power is to show its strength, whether it is hard or soft power. In other words, to understand the future relations between the United States and Russia, it is necessary to understand that the Biden Administration has placed people with long experience in key positions in the federal government, such as Antony Blinken, the Secretary of State, while President Biden himself was the Vice-President of his country for eight years. On the other hand, on the Russian side, President Putin has been in office since the early 2000s and when he left the presidency, it was to serve as head of government. As for Foreign Minister Sergey Lavrov, he has led his country's diplomacy since 2004. If

---

[8] Samuel Huntington, *The Clash of Civilizations and the Remaking of World Order*, Simon & Schuster, 1996, 367 pp.

the United States has greater means than Russia in terms of hard and soft power, Russia certainly has arguments to put forward in order not to put itself in a position of having to accept American decisions or demands without compensation. When Russia is economically sanctioned, it turns to China, rethinks its diplomacy in the Middle East, reconsiders its bilateral relations with Turkey, or broadcasts messages of concern to Western Europe and North America about its ambitions in the Arctic region.

These are just a few examples that tend to show that, in the face of the firmness shown by the United States, Russia does not lack arguments to put forward. The principle is to make it clear that Moscow will not submit to any decision without reacting. This is undoubtedly the spirit that prevailed during this meeting between heads of state. They had to meet and engage in direct dialogue rather than sending messages to each other through the media. The predictable result is that each of them took advantage of this moment to firmly address a message to his alter ego. The deal is clear: if Presidents Putin and Biden are the chief executives of their respective countries, Russian-American relations are likely to remain sensitive and even tense. It is in fact a clever balancing act that is being perpetuated, reminiscent in some respects of past episodes of the Cold War, with the difference that the opposition of yesteryear confronted two blocs and that the truth of contemporary international relations contains an additional superpower in the person of China. It is certain that Moscow will meticulously observe the evolution of Sino-American relations to adapt its positioning in relation to Washington and / or Beijing. It is all a question of calculation and in this game of chess, the Putin-Lavrov pair is without doubt the most experienced.

Effective US-European rapprochement in sight
June 2021

President Biden often says that he does not intend to govern the United States as his predecessor did, but he shares a common trait with his predecessor: both waited several months before making their first official trip. For Donald Trump, his first trip abroad was a memorable one, as his destination was Saudi Arabia, where he established a strong friendship with the Crown Prince, to whom he managed to sell several hundred billion dollar-worth of contracts, particularly in the arms industry. In the wake of this, he travelled to Israel to affirm the good diplomatic relations he intended to establish with Jerusalem, which were excellent during his four years in power. It is less well known that he then left for Belgium for a NATO summit and that he punctuated his first trip outside his national borders with the G7 summit held in Taormina, Sicily, where the Western world understood that its political and commercial relations with Washington were likely to be complicated for at least four years. Everyone remembers that Donald Trump gave priority to Saudi Arabia and Israel before sailing to Europe. The first official trip of a US head of state is always an event with a high symbolic value.

As for President Biden, he is no exception to the rule. It is after nearly five months of governance that he leaves the United States to go to Europe and more precisely to Cornwall to participate in the next G7. It is important to understand that he intends to match words with deeds: he had promised during his election campaign that his desire in terms of diplomacy was to get closer as soon as possible to the traditional allies of the United States, who were coming out of a bad experience with the unpredictable and truculent Donald Trump. The latter had always affirmed his desire to make American interests prevail at all costs, even if this was to the detriment of traditional partners. Two decisions left their mark: the withdrawal of the United States from the 2015 Paris Climate Agreement (which President Biden promptly reinstated) and Washington's disengagement from the Iranian nuclear issue to show a much more intransigent diplomatic line towards Tehran. Joe Biden wanted to undo what had been put in place by his predecessor. He had announced this during his election campaign. He quickly set out to make the diplomatic shift once he was elected and above all invested in his presidential duties. The target was obviously to renew friendly and courteous ties with the Old Continent, which had been fairly scalded by the Trump experience but also by the Brexit affair, which weakened the political and economic balance of the European Union (EU).

This Brexit affair was largely supported by Donald Trump who did not fail to publicly humiliate Theresa May by declaring in England, alongside the main interested party, that the United Kingdom should be piloted by a leader who would have no hesitation in committing to a hard Brexit ... As a reminder, Theresa May had announced her resignation from her responsibilities as Prime Minister a few days earlier, but the message of Donald Trump directed the eyes to Boris Johnson who was appointed to the head of the British government a few weeks later. All that is now history. Is it? Perhaps not as much as it may seem. Boris Johnson was known for his proximity to Donald Trump, but the Republican President's defeat in November 2020 changed the game as the former London mayor began to see growing popular discontent in his country due to the bad impact of Brexit on the lives of his fellow citizens. Some actually and bitterly regret their vote expressed yet in favor of a British withdrawal from the EU. For Boris Johnson, it is now not easy to maintain diplomatic and commercial relations with the EU without facing unfortunate consequences, not to mention the health crisis that is still not over and that continues to seriously hamper the movement of people. It is in this global context that President Biden is making his first official visit abroad. He could have traveled earlier, but he probably chose, and rightly so, to focus on the health, political and social ills that continue to plague the social balance in Uncle Sam's country. This first trip to Europe is not insignificant. It comes during a G7 meeting, but it is above all an opportunity to reiterate his firm desire to renew friendly relations with his traditional partners and to indicate to them the need for Western strength and cohesion to stand up to the foreign power clearly designated as a common enemy by Washington: not surprisingly, it is obviously China. Joe Biden did not come only to revive a diplomacy with Europe that had become strained and moribund. He clearly hopes to give impetus to a new dynamic that is collective and sustainable.

China worries. China is scary. For President Biden, it is important to put the United States back at the heart of an alliance that had faltered during the Trump era. It is imperative to return to a vision of unity as strength. The United States, alone, is vulnerable to Chinese ambitions. On the other hand, if the United States is accompanied by a whole battery of allied partners, such a front would probably be more effective in trying to thwart Beijing's ambitions. Therefore, President Biden wants to move away from isolationism and return to a constructive dialogue with Europe and other allied powers that have been scalded by the Trump experience. After the G7, German Chancellor Angela Merkel is already scheduled to visit Washington in July 2021, a few weeks before the German legislative elections. It is likely that she will make such a visit for strategic purposes. The idea is probably based on the desire to restore bilateral relations to a healthy state before she steps down as head of government. It is important in the eyes of the White House and the State Department to renew a constructive dialogue with traditional allies, to restore relations of trust, a feeling that had been severely affected during the Trump Administration. As for Angela Merkel, the idea is undoubtedly to establish a dialogue that will be continued by her successor. Indeed, it should not be overlooked that the two main European political and economic engines will soon be facing elections that may bring important changes in national and international governance. Angela Merkel's political party is not guaranteed to win the next German parliamentary elections. As for French President Emmanuel Macron, he is not certain to be re-elected in 2022 or to be followed by a parliamentary majority, if at all (the most likely hypothesis is that he will run for a second presidential term).

It is therefore important that the United States and the EU find a dialogue that will be sustainable, regardless of the electoral circumstances in Germany or France. It is often said that governing means planning. In other words, when responding to an electoral mandate, only the general interest counts. Therefore, it is important that Chancellor Merkel and President Macron establish good relations with President Biden and assure him that good relations with their respective countries will be maintained, even if there is a change of leadership.

The Covid crisis will leave its mark. Doubt is more permitted since, in the face of the hesitations of the scientific community, the hypothesis of a laboratory manipulation is not only not discarded but in the eyes of certain scientists, it is considered the most probable hypothesis. This obviously poses a problem if it was a program decided by China. The day that a definite clarification related to the mystery of the exact origin of the

Covid crisis is published, a diplomatic crisis may arise in such a case. However, it will be difficult to get another answer, this time about the deliberate intent to create a virus in the laboratory for global dissemination. Should it be determined that the origin of Covid-19 is laboratory-based, there is every reason to believe that the United States will do its best to exert continued pressure on China (diplomatically and economically), probably with the assistance of European allies. This is one of the reasons why President Biden has asked his intelligence agencies to produce a report to determine the exact origin of this form of coronavirus, which is now blamed for more than three and a half million deaths worldwide.

On the other hand, he wants to show his Republican opponents that he intends to always keep the pressure on China and that he is a staunch defender of the idea that America will maintain its political and economic leadership under his presidency. Diligent reporting by the intelligence community seems to demonstrate his desire to obtain valuable information about what the Trump Administration really knew and to determine whether there are grounds for legal action for withholding information that should have been disclosed. President Biden is playing on all fronts in his relations with China: he wants to show Xi Jinping that he is a statesman who will defend his country's interests above all else. As for the domestic scene, he is sending a message to Donald Trump and the Republican Party. In this, he knows that his European partners have bad memories of their experience with Donald Trump. Although they do not venture into American domestic policy issues, they share more of Joe Biden's diplomatic vision. Similarly, it is very likely that he, France, and Germany will be able to find a common dialogue to restart discussions on the Iranian nuclear crisis.

When it comes to the Iranian issue, it is worth remembering that there are other parties to the discussions: the United Kingdom, China, and Russia. The process was launched when Barack Obama was still the President of the United States. China and Russia agreed to find a collegial solution and thus open a multiparty dialogue that was shattered when Donald Trump was elected, eager to assert the almighty diplomatic power of the United States and make no concessions to Iran. His diplomatic vision in the Middle East had been very clear from the outset: to discuss with Saudi Arabia and Israel, two countries hostile to Iran. It was then understood that he would make no effort to pursue discussions, preferring to force a decision: to derail what had been undertaken. It was unbearable for him to consider diplomacy with Tehran. He wanted to show his determination to bring that country to heel. This very assertive vision was also intended to send a message to the other parties involved: he had succeeded in business by imposing his choices and ideas. He intended to do the same in politics. This is how he managed to undermine everything that was done to try to achieve a denuclearization of Iran. The real losers in this diplomacy were the three European states.

Indeed, as far as Russia and China are concerned, these two countries deal with Iran despite the economic sanctions... China did not hesitate during the Trump Administration in the United States to seal giant agreements for the purchase of hydrocarbons and the sale of manufactured goods. As for Russia, it has refined its relations with Iran with a view to future military cooperation... This situation, which was uncomfortable and even humiliating for London, Berlin, and Paris, was more difficult to bear because the United States maintained permanent pressure on any economic actor allied with the United States who ventured to trade with Iran. It is not surprising, moreover, that the three European states tried to revive talks with Iran because of the diplomatic relations that were becoming difficult with the Trump Administration.

President Biden has every interest in showing himself to be close to the convictions of his European partners on the Iranian issue. This is an affair that has caused a scar on the European side and that is still struggling to be definitively forgotten. From this point of view, Americans and Europeans should easily find common ground on how to conduct discussions with Iran. It would not be surprising, moreover, if China and Russia were to support a joint proposal to Tehran. Indeed, in a sensitive diplomatic context, particularly with regard to US-China relations, a multiparty agreement would have the advantage of calming all existing tensions, such as Russia-Ukraine relations, which sometimes continue to be in the news, or the Covid-19 health crisis, for which China is often singled out by the Western world as being responsible for this disease that has struck the planet for the past year and a half. Such an outcome must occur if all actors are pragmatic and realistic. We give a lot of credit to this hypothesis.

President Biden has another issue to bring to the attention of his European friends to promote a rapprochement: Russia. So far, there is nothing surprising about this, since the 46th President of the United States defends a diplomatic vision that was that of Barack Obama, of whom he was the loyal second-in-command, although since then, the political and economic rise of China has made it the number one rival of the White House and the American Administrations. The Russian dossier is more attractive because it is "easier" to attack Moscow, to be "inflexible and intractable" with the Kremlin than to opt for the same offensive strategy with China. When it comes to raising the hypothesis of military intervention in the event of a new conflict between Russia and Ukraine, the communication is obviously different when it comes to China... even if military maneuvers, for example and once again those carried out in the China Sea, are intended to show that the United States is ready to consider any kind of option, including the use of armed force, in the event of an escalation of tensions with Beijing, which does not hesitate to carry out similar maneuvers.

For Russia, the case is different. It is the ideal rival. The problem is that the Cold War has been over for three decades... but there is still a mutual distrust between Moscow and the Western world, especially with Western European countries that have continued to have tumultuous relations with the Russian capital. We are thinking first of the continuing rivalry with the United Kingdom. Recently, the Navalny affair was the latest episode in a resurgence of diplomatic tensions with the Kremlin. However, despite the reciprocal "threats" that characterize Russian-Western relations and Russia's military plans (such as its efforts to arm or militarize certain regions of the Arctic) that worry the Western world, Russia's defense budget is not comparable to that of the United States and its European allies: it is much lower, while China's has grown steadily in recent years to the point where it is now three to four times larger than Russia's.

The political agenda for the G7 participants was heavy as they had to leave English Cornwall and head to Brussels for the NATO summit. This summit was very timely as it allowed for the clarification of thorny issues within the alliance. The priorities of the heads of state and government present differed for some without being in contradiction. The only exception was Turkey, a country that has had tense diplomatic relations with the alliance for many years, particularly regarding the EU, its position on Middle East issues, and the relations that Ankara maintains with Russia.

The first lesson of this summit was the working atmosphere. It was the first summit in which President Biden participated. Initial comments indicated a more relaxed atmosphere than those to which the participants were accustomed during the four years in which the American representative was none other than Donald Trump. However, it was important for President Biden to outline what he intends to do with his allies, his vision, and his fears. Not surprisingly, he denounced the threats posed by China and Russia. The other message was *"America is back"*. It was indeed necessary to ensure that NATO regains its vigor, the lost vigor that prompted President Macron to make a blunt comment when he declared the Atlantic alliance brain-dead. [9] This rhetoric showed the growing difficulties within NATO when Donald Trump saw more disadvantages than benefits. Joe Biden resolutely turned to the option of reactivating the alliance and working together with the other twenty-nine member states. It was necessary to reassure and convince. From this point of view, he undoubtedly succeeded in his seduction operation.

However, President Macron has stated another objective: it concerns disarmament. That being the case, it is not incompatible with the American vision, since by disarmament one must understand the countries that the French President would like to target, among which are obviously the states that wish to acquire nuclear weapons. This also involves China and Russia. On the one hand, Russia worries the rest of Europe and the other states bordering the Arctic, who are not happy about the

---

[9] *"Emmanuel Macron warns Europe: NATO is becoming brain-dead"*, www.economist.com, November 7, 2019

establishment of new military bases and human presence in island regions where the climate is extremely harsh. Russia sends a message and confirms its desire to play a role in the new geopolitics of the Arctic. Russia has also made it known that it also has formidable high-tech weapons. As for China, the problem is different: its annual defense budget is constantly increasing, but its diplomatic relations with the West have become more complicated, particularly with the United States and the United Kingdom, which is also engaged in military maneuvers in the China Sea. The atmosphere is tense. China and the alliance United States-United Kingdom are testing each other, evaluating each other, showing their military muscles to intimidate or dissuade the adversary.

The objective of the Brussels summit was to confirm this diplomatic renewal desired and announced by Joe Biden during the G7, but also to ensure that NATO member states were willing to agree to defend common interests. In this respect, President Biden has succeeded in reassuring his allies and convincing them that the Trump era is over. It was now important to start again on a new solid diplomatic basis. As for the more targeted message, it is obviously unambiguous: he did not fail to designate China and Russia as embodying real threats for the whole world. This confirms above all that world geopolitics is once again undergoing a major turning point. The Western world seems to be on the way to demonstrating an unwavering alliance against Russia and especially China. In short, the scenario, as it is taking shape, was foreseeable, but it was subject to the sine qua non condition that President Biden would manage to be persuasive and unifying to initiate this new dynamic of alliance, which concerns both hard and soft power. Finally, it also shows that there are several poles of influence in the world. To put it another way, we have confirmation of a multipolar world in international relations, a trend that seems set to last. President Biden has just laid the groundwork for a new Western position in international relations. It was in the air at the time. It was confirmed in Cornwall and then in Brussels.

The thorny North Korean nuclear issue
May 2021

For several decades, North Korea has been engaged in a military nuclear program. This is a way for this isolated country on the international scene to maintain a permanent threat to the entire international community but also to establish the omnipotence of the Kim dynasty. To date, the regime in Pyongyang is playing with the nerves of the international community, including China, the traditional and unwavering ally, which is sometimes annoyed by the actions and provocations of its neighbor. North Korea is part of a great game that is fully integrated into the political and economic rivalry between the United States and China. The small communist state knows how to take advantage of this geopolitical situation to pursue its military policy despite diplomatic and economic sanctions. Many state actors are showing their fear. South Korea and Japan are geographically on the front line and are concerned about the ballistic and nuclear tests of this neighbor that continues to provoke.

As for the United States, the country designated as the great enemy of the *Juche*-oriented [10] regime, an admission of impotence has been made. Donald Trump tried to engage in discussions with Kim Jong-Un while the beginnings of the 45th American President in history suggested conflicting relations, particularly through an

---

[10] Author's note: *Juche* is a doctrine promoted by Kim Il-Sung and could be translated as "self-sufficiency". It takes up communist thought in its broad lines, but with some characteristics of its own which distinguish it from Marxist and Leninist theses. He explained that he understood new revolutionary principles and defended a new vision of sovereignty. In his vision, reunification with South Korea was to be achieved. This word was first uttered by Kim Il-Sung in a speech at a political convention in 1955. This doctrine has mainly enabled him to establish absolute power in North Korea.

official communication that was intended to be uncompromising and without concession: North Korea would, willingly or not, bend to the demands of the White House and be forced to denuclearize. It was a lost cause. Unexpectedly, a dialogue was opened between Donald Trump and Kim Jong-Un, and two meetings were even held to discuss the scenario of North Korea's denuclearization. Donald Trump never hid his confidence that the Pyongyang regime would accept the proposed conditions... which turned out to be a real failure and a slap in the face for American diplomacy. At the time, Donald Trump's advisors strongly advised against engaging in discussions with Kim Jong-Un, fearing, rightly, that the latter could play the American President at the time.

Several hypotheses can be envisaged to achieve relative tranquility vis-à-vis North Korea. Until now, all the scenarios imagined have never led to a concrete result except to increase the pressure through diplomatic and economic sanctions. Most of North Korea's income is spent on its national defense budget. In the West, the perception of this country is that of a state where part of the population lives in very precarious conditions. However, its military arsenal is frightening. Despite this, North Korea manages to circumvent certain sanctions and to secure revenues. On the other hand, China helps its neighbor by providing most of its energy needs as well as other aid (food and medical in particular) which allows it to maintain the Kim family in power. Indeed, between the United States and China, the main issue is to keep the Kim family in power. Despite North Korea's actions, which are sometimes disapproved of by China, there is no question of risking a change in the ruling elites and seeing American troops being able to move closer to China's borders. North Korea acts as a buffer state in a region where the United States has strategic allies, namely South Korea and Japan. These two countries constantly fear that Pyongyang will slip up. The possibility of an accidental outbreak of war cannot be ruled out. It is indeed possible that a North Korean military maneuver could accidentally impact South Korea or Japan and that this would lead to an immediate response. Ballistic launches have already been carried out from North Korean territory and crossed South Korean and Japanese airspace without authorization. To put it plainly, North Korea is playing with fire.

However, this strategy is not insignificant since both countries are allies of the United States and the history of the 20th century in this part of the Far East is full of reasons for North Korea to consider South Korea and Japan as enemies of the nation. The regional climate is therefore very unstable, and sensitivities are high. At present, it is unlikely that North Korea will change course. There is every reason to believe that it will continue its policy of provocation towards the international community, as this is what allows its leaders to ensure their continued power. However, there is a segment of the national population that is undoubtedly eager for change, as living conditions are very harsh, but another segment gives unwavering and unconditional support to its elites. In a country where everything is strictly controlled by the state, North Koreans must surely consider the risks to themselves and their families if they were to stand up against the system. The consequences for them would be dire. Yet, the country's military arsenal must be considered and international efforts to try to "solve" the North Korean issue must continue. This is the subject of our reflection.

An isolated and warmongering confetti in the Far East
The survival of the North Korean regime depends on its military program. It has a dual function: to ensure the Kim family's control over the country and to convince the

national population of its military omnipotence aimed at exacerbating a nationalism that, accompanied by permanent indoctrination and an authoritarianism that some analysts describe as totalitarianism, manages to overcome the social and food crises that Pyongyang faces while the regime does not seem to be exposed to socio-political destabilization. In a system where almost everything seems to be controlled, any form of dissent must be matured before any action is taken because of the many consequences that any individual or family may suffer afterwards. Seeking to leave the country is a serious act. Those who cross the border illegally do so at the risk of their lives. If they fail, they know that they will be sentenced to hard labor or even execution, while their families will also suffer the wrath of the regime. North Korean political refugees are rare, and their testimonies are also rare. They never speak openly in the media for fear of reprisals against their family members back home. Such a political system can only be perpetuated by the imposition of a regime of terror. The Kim dynasty understood this well and this from the time Kim Il-Sung came to power in 1948.

The big idea was to exploit Kim Il-Sung's immense popularity among the national population to establish a personality cult and give him a quasi-divine existence. Indeed, the personality cult was continued for his successor and then his grandson Kim Jong-Un. The Kim dynasty has been "deified" to the point that many historical inconsistencies are littered in the propaganda communication. For example, it has been officially admitted that Kim Jong-Il (Kim Il-Sung's son and Kim Jong-Un's father) played an important role in the fight against the Japanese during World War II even though he was born in the early 1940s. All this mythology contributes to the indoctrination of the population, which obviously does not have access to sufficient means of communication to understand everything that is happening outside the country's borders. For several decades, the United States has been perceived as an enemy of the nation (as has Japan for other reasons). It is up to the country's leaders to convince the population of this "national truth" and to show that North Korea can fight any American aggression thanks to the quality of its army and its equipment. This is the reason for the many military parades in Pyongyang: to show military strength, to intimidate and remind every individual that the state will always surpass any citizen.

The North Korean regime is totalitarian in the sense that everything is under control while the individual is erased in favor of the collective. Individual indifference is indeed one of the prerogatives of totalitarian regimes. On the other hand, to establish the durability of the power in place, the regime designated enemies of the nation to mobilize the population, to keep it in a permanent state of alert, while taking care to work on the exacerbation of nationalism with a recurrent propaganda on the national necessity to prepare for war. In addition to this, there is the political and logistical support of China, which has allowed the Kim dynasty to rule North Korea for over seven decades. The strength of the Pyongyang regime is that it has succeeded in developing an effective weapons program that is capable of inspiring fear. The fantasy (or eccentricity) of certain decisions or communications leaves the impression that Pyongyang could commit the irreparable at any moment.

However, it would probably not be in North Korea's interest to start a war with neighboring South Korea or Japan without exposing itself to a large-scale retaliation, especially since such an aggression would certainly imply an American military intervention, a scenario that would obviously not please China. While the risk of war is relatively low, although specialists in Korean issues consider the unpredictability and even irrationality of the North Korean leadership, one provocation too many could trigger a regional conflagration at any time. Warmongering is an integral part of the ingredients the Kim family needs to control, mobilize, and intimidate the population. Such a discourse has a double significance: firstly, externally, since it is addressed to the "enemies of the nation"; and secondly, internally, insofar as it is intended to "reassure" the population while conveying the message of the unshakeable strength of the ruling elites. This is the most obvious expression of *hard power*, which is the only real asset available to the Kim family, but which is sufficient to avoid being exposed to high risks of internal unrest.

Despite its isolation on the international scene and the diplomatic and economic sanctions, North Korea manages, year after year, to perpetuate a "national political tradition" that began in the late 1940s and which appears to be an incongruity in the Western world... but which is so precious to China, especially in view of the growing rivalry between it and the United States. At the end of the hostilities of the Korean War, which is still technically not over, the United States has so far always failed to make North Korea understand that it is not working to develop a nuclear program for military purposes. In Pyongyang, nuclear weapons have always been seen as a means of breaking free from American control.

A constant haunt for American allies in the region
The North Korean leader gives the impression of wanting to play with the Western world. In his communication strategy, there is almost a childish dimension. Indeed, the state propaganda likes to show military parades and exhibitions of high-tech weapons to impress the North Korean people but also to send a message

of international significance. In the region, the two main American allies are Japan and South Korea. It is an understatement to say that Tokyo and Seoul are still afraid of an "accident". In this case, Pyongyang's provocations can indeed and accidentally lead to tragedy if a ballistic missile strikes Japanese or South Korean territory. There are violations of the airspace of these two countries, and in the event of a major incident, we are not convinced that diplomacy would succeed in resolving such a dispute. The climate is always extremely sensitive.

As for South Korea, the war that started in the 1950s is technically not over. It is the oldest conflict still alive in the world. As for Japan, North Korean resentment is linked to the history of the 20th century when troops from the Land of the Rising Sun invaded the Korean peninsula and mistreated the indigenous people. Finally, the fact that these two states are close to the Western world is reminiscent of the war context that forever split Korea into two state entities, one supported by the United States and the other by the surrounding communist states. Since then, the North Korean regime has relied on propaganda communication to show the benefits of communism while naming the enemies of the nation for whom the people must always be prepared to fight. This is how North Korea has built up an army that is disproportionately large in relation to its national population. It is also with this idea in mind that the regime devotes a large part of its resources to research, development, and the acquisition of weapons.

In the West, it is difficult to understand the personality of Kim Jong-Un. However, he has been personally connected to Western life. During his youth, he was taken to study at a Swiss school under a false identity. This life experience enabled him to learn foreign languages and to become familiar with the Western world. It was in

Switzerland that he developed a boundless passion for basketball, especially the North American NBA championship. When he was appointed by his father as the future number one of the regime, he was not yet thirty years old and he certainly had to ensure the loyalty of the army. Thus, he quickly imposed his style by deploying a ruthless policy and adopting a look like that of Kim Il-Sung, the tutelary figure of the nation with a haircut reminiscent of that of his late grandfather and which he is the only one allowed to wear in North Korea, employing the same mimetics or gestures and recalling repeatedly the almost deified dimension of his grandfather. It was announced that Kim Jong-Un had personally ordered the execution of his uncle, who was the number two in the regime. This execution was intended to act as an electroshock for anyone who might not obey Kim Jong-Un's orders.

The indoctrination of the national population but especially all the propaganda articulated around the military means and the ballistic and nuclear tests irritate the South Korean and Japanese neighbors. These incessant provocations are not without risks. The slightest serious incident is likely to trigger hostilities for which a ripple effect would certainly be activated. Indeed, the scenario of a war cannot be ruled out if South Korean or Japanese territory is hit even accidentally. The United States would lend a hand to South Korea and Japan. It would then be likely that China would give its "support" to North Korea. By support, one should understand logistical assistance that would be reminiscent of the Cold War, a period during which the USSR and the United States never directly confronted each other. When one of the two superpowers was directly involved in an armed conflict, the other provided logistical support to the opposing side. This would be the most likely scenario, but it would pose a serious threat to the global geopolitical balance. It is undeniable that North Korean provocations are not without risk and should not be underestimated because of the snowball effect they can induce.

However, through these recurrent provocations, the North Korean regime is consolidating its hold on the country and ensuring the "loyalty" of its people, a large part of whom are convinced that the Western world is really an enemy of the North Korean nation. To endure, the dynasty must continue to maintain this permanent climate of threat because it is a "legitimization" of the continuation of the struggle against the Western enemies. This is how the regime manages to mobilize the people while distilling a permanent propaganda in this direction with the sanctions foreseen for any recalcitrant individual. North Korean totalitarianism relies on a warmongering policy to better control the system from inside.

Kim Jong-Un, the skillful negotiator
He reigns over North Korea by imposing force and terror, but in the past, he has been able to put on a show to ease tensions. As in the spirit of the Cold War, there was a period of détente during which the Western world was challenged by Kim Jong-Un's "docility" to engage in dialogue with his domestic enemies. We remember the diplomatic rapprochement with neighboring South Korea in the run-up to the 2018 PyeongChang Olympics when it was even decided that the women's ice hockey team would be shared by both Koreas. There were gestures and signs of appeasement, but the whole question lays in the sustainability of such an initiative.

A few months after the Olympic deadline, the first meeting between Kim Jong-Un and Donald Trump took place, resulting in an unreal communication plan in which the two heads of state seemed to have forged a true friendship. The praise was mutual, and everything led to believe that the future of North Korea would be placed under the seal of pacifism, that the hatchet left due to old demons would be definitively buried. This was not the case. Donald Trump overestimated his ability to achieve a resounding diplomatic success where many of his predecessors never managed to achieve a lasting peace with North Korea. He thought he could use his business skills to bend his opponent into submission, which would inevitably end the Kim dynasty in Pyongyang. It was certain that China would never have validated such a scenario. Yet, despite the advice of his Administration, President Trump committed himself to the denuclearization of North Korea without concession, confident in his strength and persuasiveness. Washington's diplomatic shift was a mistake. It was widely criticized afterwards by John Bolton (he was the National Security advisor during the Trump Administration) and rightly so.

Kim Jong-Un has managed to play the Western world. He never intended to denuclearize his country, knowing that such an operation would certainly weaken his position in North Korea. His strike force is the main argument for keeping him in power. It was therefore foreseeable that Donald Trump's diplomatic maneuver would be a failure. The winner of these negotiations is clearly Kim Jong-Un, who was able to show the world the face of a cunning man in the face of Donald Trump's blind determination. He let the American President come to him to better trap him. Until proven otherwise, the real estate tycoon cannot claim to have achieved diplomatic success. He is aware of this but does not admit it. For him, it was necessary to make the effort to meet Kim Jong-Un and exchange with him, but he forgets that he was committed to obtaining the total denuclearization of North Korea. Meanwhile, the Pyongyang regime has never stopped, let alone ceased, its military nuclear program. The verdict is clear: Kim Jong-Un has won his duel with Donald Trump.

The election of Joe Biden has helped to revive Pyongyang's official warmongering communication. By doing so, Kim Jong-Un is setting the rules of the game with the United States by maintaining a permanent threat, understanding that the White House and the State Department will only be able to carry out a military intervention if and only if North Korea were to commit the irreparable. The discourse has changed radically since the departure of Donald Trump. That said, when he was inaugurated President in January 2017, his first comments regarding North Korea were not marked by pacifism. The first exchanges even led to fears of the worst. Donald Trump did not hesitate to call the North Korean leader a *"rocket man"*, a *"psychopath"* or a *"fat kid"*. When tensions eased and the plan for a bilateral meeting began to take shape, the relationship between the two men changed forever.

The first meeting had the surprising result of showing two men who seemed to share a budding friendship. The same spirit animated the second meeting in Hanoi a year later, even though President Trump had previously displayed his impatience with North Korea's good faith in denuclearizing. It must be recognized that he has tackled a problem for which the strategy employed was not the right one. This is the main observation that emerges from this approach. Kim Jong-Un has been able to take a wait-and-see attitude and to give the impression that he is doing something right in terms of communication. His seduction operation worked with Donald Trump. He was able to seduce without giving in return what was expected by the other side. However, this scenario was predictable. In this case, North Korea has never had the intention to start a denuclearization process. Despite President Trump's efforts, the Pyongyang regime remains a thorn in the side of the White House, the US State Department, South Korea, and Japan.

The American impasse or the status quo

Hypotheses to bend North Korea towards denuclearization of the country are very unlikely since the Pyongyang regime relies on this force as a means of pressure to keep this weapon without having to make any concessions. North Korea is already heavily sanctioned but still manages to generate revenues that allow it to survive year after year. For the United States and its regional allies, there is a great desire to see North Korea switch to another political regime and to see the Kim family removed from power. However, how can this be achieved without exposing oneself to a reaction from Pyongyang? On the other hand, if the United States is successful in this regard, how would China react to a radical change of governance in North Korea? Although international relations and diplomacy are not exact sciences, it would be surprising if North Korean governance were to change any time soon unless it were to come from within, which also seems unlikely given the risks to the people of insubordination.

A US military intervention can only be envisaged in the event of a North Korean attack. This is the only case in which we can reasonably envisage such an outcome. This would imply that the maneuver would be the result of a reaction, i.e., a North Korean attack or any accidental action or maneuver striking the United States or an American ally. This would be the most likely hypothesis. In the face of an attack, even an accidental one, one should expect an armed response in return. If a North Korean strike were to hit a power under the U.S. umbrella, there is no doubt that the response would be ruthless. Although Pyongyang's official communication has once again turned hawkish and the provocations have never ceased, Kim Jong-Un has no interest in crossing the line of no return that would inevitably lead to an armed conflict. While China supports its neighbor, it does not tolerate all provocations by Pyongyang, precisely because it fears that an ill-managed action could lead to armed conflict.

A war involving North Korea is obviously not desirable. North Korea's weaponry is good, but a foreign coalition led by the United States would probably have a good chance of carrying out targeted and effective strikes to neutralize strategic installations. Pyongyang's nuisance power is great and could cause significant damage in South Korea or Japan, or even in the United States. Missile shields are not immune to strikes. They can neutralize some missiles but not all in the case of a massive attack. In the case of armed opposition, North Korea can indeed cause damage but would probably have great difficulty in containing enemy strikes. The chances are that the dynastic regime would not survive such a retaliation... unless China intervenes in turn. This would mean direct armed opposition between Washington and Beijing. We refuse to believe in such a hypothesis because the consequences would not only be increased but could also be out of control.

From our point of view, the most credible hypothesis is that of a status quo. In other words, barring an unlikely domestic uprising, the Kim dynasty is likely to continue to reign supreme despite rumors that Kim Jong-Un is in poor health. The Biden Administration will no doubt continue to have to "take" Pyongyang's hawkish messages, as the United States naturally remains North Korea's sworn enemy. However, President Biden does not rule out the idea of a meeting with Kim Jong-Un, but if it were to take place, it would certainly not be based on the kind of communication that Donald Trump once conducted. Similarly, the United States and South Korea are joining forces to establish a common technological front. The purpose of this partnership is twofold: first, to send a message to China; second, to show North Korea as well that the U.S.-South Korean partnership is solid.

On the American side, the Biden Administration's strategy is being implemented, patiently, knowing full well that there is little room for maneuver if Pyongyang continues to enjoy Beijing's support. It is now up to North Korea not to commit the irreparable to risk a violent response. Western analysts are questioning Kim Jong-Un's sanity, fearing that he may one day carry out his threats and attack the United States or its allies. While we do not underestimate the North Korean leader, we note that the official discourse has remained unchanged for several decades, even though North Korea has nuclear weapons, and as such, it is preferable not to underestimate the risks. It is obviously desirable that he never be tempted to use nuclear weapons... The only certainty we have is that in the event of a direct dialogue between Kim Jong-Un and Joe Biden, the American diplomatic approach would be different from that of Donald Trump.

Cold war atmosphere and Chinese shadow
This is not a revelation, but without Chinese help, it is very likely that the North Korean regime would not have been able to survive for so long under such sanctions. Make no mistake: the arsenal of sanctions, in the Western view, is aimed at weakening the omnipotence of the Kim family. The goal is a change in political governance. To this end, China seeks a permanent balance when sanctions are voted on in the UN Security Council: not to antagonize other voters while approving sanctions that are not too damaging

to the political balance of its neighbor. China needs North Korea, and North Korea is playing it up as part of its hawkish communication towards the United States and its allies.

However, bilateral political relations between Beijing and Pyongyang are sometimes turbulent because of the liberties taken by North Korea, which can at any moment generate a renewed crisis or even a shift to armed conflict in the worst-case scenario. The Chinese leaders sometimes show irritation close to anger in the face of the recurrent provocations of their "little brother". The major difficulty is that of maintaining a balance in relations. The Kim dynasty would obviously be threatened without Chinese help, and conversely, keeping this family in power ensures that China has a buffer state that separates it from its American allies. For Beijing, it is therefore unthinkable that the regime in Pyongyang could be threatened and that it would lead to a change in political governance that would allow the United States to extend its area of influence and move closer to China's borders. Relations between Beijing and Pyongyang have been tensed at times, but for several decades any tension has been punctuated by an inevitable return to a calmer bilateral relationship. Each needs the other.

The American dream is to see the fall of the Kim family and the abandonment of the *Juche* doctrine, the rule that regulates the functioning of the country and that takes into consideration a quasi-deification of its leaders, including the founder of the North Korean republic Kim Il-Sung. China continues its support because its neighbor is upsetting American diplomacy as well as that of its allies. South Korea is in the front line because it shares borders with the Northern part of the peninsula. Seoul is only about fifty kilometers from the North Korean border and is obviously not reassured when Pyongyang communicates threatening messages. However, it is certain that any North Korean strike on South Korea would lead to a regional conflagration. It would rekindle the old war between the two sides, which has never legally ended since 1953.

When we talk about 1953, we are referring to that deadly conflict, which was in fact one of the first confrontations of the Cold War. Today, we find this spirit again insofar as the Sino-American rivalry has since supplanted the American-Soviet opposition of the past. North Korea is taking advantage of this situation more than ever to blow hot and cold with its recurrent provocations. Many of these provocations have the approval of China, which does not accept provocations that are too risky and can lead to uncontrolled consequences. However, since he took over the leadership of his country, Kim Jong-Un has shown that he is capable of being attentive to Beijing's recommendations. Prior to the two meetings in which he exchanged views with Donald Trump, he had made trips to China to "take advice" from his valuable allies. For a statesman who almost never leaves his country, these trips to China were naturally intended to receive advice or even more. Indeed, if the official communication showed Kim Jong-Un with the highest Chinese dignitaries smiling, relaxed and complicit, it would be more accurate to speak of instructions provided by China. Clearly, when Donald Trump was certain that he could bend North Korea through diplomacy, China seized the opportunity to lead him into a field littered with traps, including that of saving time. Kim Jong-Un played his part admirably, knowing how to give the impression that his character would seduce the volcanic Donald Trump, but sufficiently cunning not to concede anything concrete and to make evasive promises that will never be kept.

If North Korea has played the American 45th President, we must consider that China has done the same. The issue of the denuclearization of North Korea was a diplomatic victory for China, which in fact humiliated Donald Trump, who had also incurred the wrath of his close diplomatic advisers. The latter had previously advised him against engaging in such a dialogue with Kim Jong-Un. Donald Trump and Kim Jong-Un played. The second one won. However, the situation has since changed somewhat with the election of Joe Biden, who has assured his country that he intends to continue the work of opposition with China, aware that American domination is waning as its rival grows in power, both in terms of hard and soft power. North Korea will inevitably be a non-negligible player in the Sino-American rivalry. It is therefore to be expected that it will continue its tireless work of undermining the United States and its allies by blowing hot and cold.

Mutual pressure tactics

This is one of the reasons why we believe in the thesis of a neutralization or prolongation of a situation that has already existed for a long time regarding the nuclearization of North Korea. Both China and the United States have leverage. The most recent example is President Biden's desire to demand that his intelligence services submit a detailed report on the true origins of Covid-19. [11] The latter did not fail to specify that *"the United States will continue to work with its partners around the world to pressure China to participate in a complete, transparent, and evidence-based international investigation."* [12] The purpose of the maneuver is explained by the highest American authority; the idea is to determine if the origin of Covid-19 does not come from a laboratory. This thesis has

---

[11] *"Origine du Covid : Biden demande aux services de renseignement un rapport sous 90 jours"*, www.lefigaro.fr, May 26, 2021
[12] *Ibid.* Translation done by the author from French quote.

been around for a while, since it was very strongly defended when Donald Trump was still in charge of the executive branch of the United States. Should it be proven that the origin is laboratory, whether accidental or part of an agreed research program to develop bacteriological weapons, Sino-American relations could take a new turn. Moreover, President Biden will have to perform a balancing act, as he was the Vice-President of his country when American funds were allegedly used to finance in part the research activities of certain scientific laboratories located in the Wuhan region.

Diplomatic relations between the United States and China are difficult. Each side tries to destabilize the other with tariffs, scandals about espionage or immorality, and other ploys designed to antagonize the other side. However, despite all these obstacles, trade relations between the two countries are not bad: the United States needs Chinese products and services and vice versa. There is no doubt that President Biden's request is the latest in a long line of pressure tactics to put China in the bad role of the villain who has been doing unmentionable things in the greatest secrecy and who did not inform anyone when an incident was discovered. This would obviously be a terrible slap in the face for Beijing as well as for the WHO, whose credibility in the international community would suddenly be damaged by suspicion of complacency towards China. For all that, this situation of probable unrest in the making is good for North Korea, even if the major maneuvers undertaken and promoted by Joe Biden with South Korea seem to indicate that everything is being thought out to increase the pressure on the Pyongyang regime from a distance.

The Americans and South Koreans are intensifying their alliance through a common front with a technological scope aimed at antagonizing China. However, any new cooperation between Seoul and Washington is likely to antagonize Pyongyang. State propaganda is expected to castigate this new cooperation to further fuel North Korean nationalism. Once again, the observation for Washington is implacable: if the idea is to always reinforce the means of pressure towards North Korea, any intervention or incursion on North Korean soil is to be excluded under pain of North Korean reprisals and a possible Chinese intervention. In other words, an armed intervention can only be envisaged in case of North Korean aggression. As for infiltration operations to try to create a form of internal subversion, they are very risky while they do not guarantee any effectiveness. Thus, we lean towards the status quo thesis: the United States and China are jousting from a distance, sometimes on dangerous grounds such as the military maneuvers carried out by both sides in the China Sea. As far as the North Korean issue is concerned, the context between the two superpowers argues for the continuation of nuclear activities without any denuclearization program being imposed. It is therefore up to Kim Jong-Un not to commit the irreparable, the act that would definitively set the world on fire.

North Korea is likely to see the Kim dynasty continue its reign despite rumors of its supreme leader's failing health. Rumors are indeed rife that Kim Jong-Un has already prepared his succession should his health no longer allow him to carry out the demands of power. According to the South Korean intelligence services, his sister has been designated to take over in the event of the premature death of Kim Il-Sung's grandson. It is difficult to obtain reliable information as the North Korean regime keeps everything under wraps. Everything is therefore a matter of speculation. However, it is undeniable that Pyongyang has military arguments and especially weapons to put forward.

They are in themselves a kind of brake on any kind of external desire. Moreover, by acting in this way, North Korea is playing the role of a shield for China regarding the American presence in South Korea and Japan. All these elements point to a scenario in which North Korea cannot be expected to back down from its nuclear ambitions.

Conclusion

Can we envisage a diplomatic solution that is sustainable? It is with a question that we begin this conclusion. As things stand, we are tempted to answer no. Diplomacy risks systematically running up against obstacles that it will not be able to overcome. First, given the US-China rivalry, we are skeptical that UN diplomacy can work properly to resolve a long-running issue. The two great rivals are members of the permanent Security Council, and each has the right to veto. If the Security Council were to decide on new sanctions that China would find unacceptable, China would be expected to use its veto power. So far, China has already voted in favor of UN sanctions against North Korea, but only if it considers them acceptable. In this sense, if the United States were to push for a strengthening of the arsenal of sanctions against the small buffer state, China could oppose it and block further discussions on the subject. Thus, it seems to us that UN diplomacy may be powerless if it does not continue its efforts to exert permanent pressure on the Pyongyang regime to avoid the outbreak of a new war. If Kim Jong-Un continues to enjoy the unwavering support of his Chinese neighbor, he has no reason to denuclearize his country. The nuclear weapon helps to keep him in place. It is his main asset. He therefore has no intention of sacrificing it unless China orders him to do so, which seems unlikely.

It is a real war of nerves between the United States and China on the North Korean issue. Washington would like to resolve this issue as soon as possible and definitively eliminate any form of threat. As for Beijing, the idea is to see its rival getting impatient and angry over this issue which has hardly changed for several decades, except in the direction of North Korea which is constantly improving its military equipment. The Biden Administration's room for maneuver thus seems very limited. Rather than favoring dialogue, which, to the credit of the United States, has never been intended to be constructive on the side of North Korea, it would be better to go for diplomatic appeasement. We have seen this during the Trump presidency: although the former president undoubtedly made mistakes in communication, attempting to engage with Pyongyang is not an easy exercise. Kim Jong-Un played with Donald Trump and probably never had the desire to engage in real discussions aimed at denuclearizing his country. What could he have gotten in return? Probably nothing, since Donald Trump had set himself the goal of bringing North Korea to heel... which was a very poor assessment of the situation, not to mention an astounding candor at such a decision-making level.

The main fear remains the uncertainty of what Kim Jong-Un intends to do. Is he only motivated by a spirit of provocation, or does he intend to do something irreparable one day? Here again, we have our own opinion on the matter. We believe that he is playing with the Western world and that he is pleased to see the reactions of the West to every ballistic missile or nuclear test. He defies the world to better control his country. This is a political communication strategy that officially addresses other actors than those who are really targeted, in this case the North Korean people. He plays with the nationalistic feelings of his compatriots while maintaining a permanent climate of fear. This is how he manages to establish his position as the undisputed leader. The message must be sent that anyone who does not comply with his wishes will be subject to severe punishment. By provoking the world with his military arsenal, he is above all addressing his own people: the state will always be stronger than the individual. The weapons can be used against any enemy, whether outside North Korea or inside. Indeed, to maintain such totalitarian rigor, propaganda must always send messages warning against possible misbehavior. This is how fear spreads among the population, each one fearing that his or her life will be turned upside down by a simple denunciation, even if unfounded. We come to another extreme: the one who wants to do too much to show that he is blameless in the eyes of the regime. The North Korean system is based on an organized stultification of the national population which originates in the reign of terror. By "dumbing down" we mean the oppression of the people who have far too few means to even begin to make a semblance of a revolt against the established system. Yet, if the United States were to succeed in solving the North Korean nuclear problem, the solution might lie in the hypothesis of an internal political overthrow and that the people dare to challenge authority. Once again, this hypothesis seems unlikely given the instruments of repression available. North Korea has the largest army in the world in relation to its national population. Even if an internal uprising were to upset the country's internal political balance, China would probably oppose the United States and its Western allies coming to offer their help for a political transition...

Chinese support for its neighbor North Korea is long-standing. Even at a time when there was no rivalry over global economic leadership, China never wanted American troops stationed too close to its borders. Since then, the Asian giant has experienced a very dynamic economic growth to the point of making it the most serious competitor to the challenge of American domination in terms of hard and soft power. It is certain that Beijing has no desire to witness a profound political upheaval in North Korea that would allow the United States to move ever closer to its national borders and thus expand its zone of influence in the Far East. Yet, in the face of North Korea's improving military arsenal, the United States will have to deploy subtle and deft diplomacy. *"Washington will likely have to take the first step and force itself to use diplomacy as a weapon to avoid a confrontation with Pyongyang while reassuring its East Asian alliances, such as Japan and South Korea, about its ability to maintain regional stability."* [13] We agree with this thought even more because we do not see the point of North Korea making the first move. Such a move would be surprising. Pyongyang clearly has no intention of opening to the world.

Certainly, the Kim family and the regime's top officials may be eager to break free from some of the harsh economic sanctions, but not at the cost of denuclearizing the country. If North Korea were to take a first step, we would question the sincerity of the approach: would it not be a trap? A second option would be a deterioration of relations with China, which would push Pyongyang to turn immediately to other partners... The hypothesis is not very credible, and we might as well say that in such a case, we would probably see the end of the Kim era at the head of North Korea. If the United States wants to obtain something from North Korea and not only denuclearization, the Americans will have to be the first to come forward. President Biden has not ruled out this possibility and is

---

[13] Jérôme le Carrou, *"La stratégie de militarisation nord-coréenne à l'épreuve de la nouvelle administration américaine"*, www.iris-france.org, February 5, 2021 Translation done by the author from French quote.

particularly cautious about his vision of the North Korean issue.

If we summarize all the hypotheses raised, it goes without saying that Washington will have to be patient if Pyongyang does not make an unforgivable mistake. It is up to the Biden Administration to identify the best strategy to adopt to succeed in first calming the climate of tension and to ensure that Pyongyang's official communication is less bellicose in the future. This would be a first encouraging sign. As for the denuclearization of the country, it is not reasonably on the agenda. It is not part of Kim Jong-Un's plans, and if he were to do so, he would be sawing off the branch of the tree on which he is sitting. Such an assumption does not make sense. The United States can always look for ways to push through new economic sanctions to further strangle the long-suffering North Korean economy. In such a case, one should not expect to see a softening of North Korea's official communication towards Uncle Sam's country. The room for maneuver of the White House and the State Department seems to be reduced when North Korea does not show any intention or willingness to engage in a dialogue without playing tricks. Even if it were to play the sincerity card, Beijing's shadow would still hang over the Washington-Pyongyang talks. In this sense, the diplomacy deployed by Donald Trump in his time does not favor the work that awaits the Biden Administration. Although initially devoid of tact and diplomacy, the Kim Jong-Un-Donald Trump relationship surprised the world when it took on a quasi-amicable tone... except that the North Korean leader played with his American counterpart.

President Biden understood that it was useless to provoke a meeting with someone he knows will be turned down if the issue at stake is denuclearization. It will therefore be necessary to think of the diplomatic approach differently if a meeting between the two men were to take place. In the run-up to the 2018 Winter Olympics in PyeongChang, the two Koreas had temporarily resumed a dialogue that hinted at an evolution in Kim Jong-Un's diplomatic vision, which later returned to a much stricter and firmer stance. Until now, the North Korean leader has shown that he is not someone who can be easily influenced, let alone manipulated. To date, he has no reason to accede to American wishes. China will not object. On the contrary, although it is sometimes irritated by its neighbor, it is making sure that it does not make too many mistakes and that the domino effect is not triggered by the United States and its allies.

Israel-Palestine, the eternal re-start
May 2021

The tone of this reflection will be one of mood. In May 2021, a new tragic episode shakes the Middle East and more precisely the State of Israel opposed to the Palestinian Authority. The human toll is terrible: many victims on both sides, the Palestinian side being more severely affected. Once again, a new peak of tension has been reached between these two long-time enemies in arms. Once again, the international community seems helpless in the face of an escalation of tensions that could spiral out of control at any moment. There are many interests at stake, but beyond understanding what Israel and Palestine are defending, the first observation that must be made is that of a deliberate failure of diplomacy. This is not a failure on the part of the United Nations, but a deliberate American desire to oppose an intervention by the Security Council. It is more in this attitude that we must decipher what is really at stake, because ultimately, it is the entire geopolitics of the Middle East that is at the heart of the issues, confirming at the same time that international relations have become a very complex discipline of analysis, since everything is likely to evolve at a very high speed, to the point where it becomes relevant to ask the following question: what value can be given from now on to a diplomatic agreement that is supposedly qualified as historic? At the heart of the issues, the American support for Prime Minister Netanyahu is very revealing: all the diplomacy put in place by Donald Trump by wishing to recognize the diplomatic relations between Israel and certain Arab states in the region risks shattering when the main reason for this rapprochement was based on a rivalry over a common enemy: Iran.

To date, what had "brought together" in 2020 the State of Israel and several Arab powers, including Saudi

Arabia, seems to be in question since these agreements were perceived by the Palestinians as a form of abandonment by the Arab allies, while Riyadh has recently been forced to review its diplomatic position towards Tehran. The main danger remains that everything that is happening is like buildings that are ready to collapse because they are not built on solid foundations. This view is all the truer given that the United States intends to play a major role in the Middle East: The Crown Prince has been pushed to review his Iranian sensibilities against a backdrop of American pressure, and the Israeli armed intervention is endorsed by Washington in view of the role played by the American capital in the United Nations Security Council. A strategy is being deployed. There is no doubt about it. But is it under control? Nothing is less certain.

The exacerbation of new Israeli-Palestinian tensions is the result of a telescoping of several factors. The conflict in the Sheikh Jarrah neighborhood of East Jerusalem has reignited tensions in an environment where religious Zionists are seeking to buy up property from Palestinians to geographically remove them and "Judaize" the area. Second, Palestinians were forbidden to gather at the Damascus Gate as part of the Ramadan festivities. Then there were the scuffles at the Mosque Esplanade. These events influenced young Arabs in Jerusalem to take to the streets in support of the Palestinian people. All this contributed to the formation of a new crisis. Finally, there were the rocket attacks by Hamas, which claims to be the defender of the Palestinian people and wishes to supplant Fatah in this role. These rocket attacks in the direction of Israel led to an adverse response. As a rule, there are persistent issues that can lead to a sudden flare-up at any time. Israel fears for its national security regarding Hamas' activities. The Palestinian Authority wants to get out of a situation it does not accept. However, recognition of an independent state is not on the agenda. There are many reasons for the quarrels, and with each new escalation of tensions, it is feared that the situation will degenerate to a point of no return. Indeed, if direct opposition pits these two hostile neighbors against each other, any new and lasting crisis is likely to spread over space and no longer be confined to the borders of Israel and Palestine, especially in a regional environment already plagued by many long-lasting crises that cannot be resolved. There have been heated moments in the past, but this time there is a fear that the confrontations will last longer or even escalate in intensity. Polemology is not an exact science. Conflict science analyses are often undermined by the appearance of unexpected disruptive elements that change the nature of an issue. In this case, the actors likely to influence the evolution of the situation are numerous. While it is not possible to list them all, the United States, the United Nations, and the Arab powers in the region can effectively seek to ease tensions or, conversely, to exacerbate them. Indeed, not everything rests exclusively on Israeli and Palestinian wills: there are certainly external influences.

The Israel-Hamas confrontation has probably already produced a winner: Prime Minister Netanyahu. He has struggled for a long time to form a new government, and the current clashes will help him to organize a coalition to enable him to form a government team from the negotiated parliamentary majority. As for the main loser, we point to US President Joe Biden. From our point of view, he has contributed to this new disorder in the Middle East, but it is a very risky position to have blocked the United Nations Security Council. Indeed, by doing so, he intends to send a message to Russia and China in particular, but above all he is taking a huge risk by torpedoing the diplomacy put in place by his predecessor who had worked for a rapprochement between Israel, the United Arab

Emirates and Saudi Arabia among others. While a diplomatic agreement seemed unlikely given the long-standing enmities characterizing relations between the Israeli state and the regional Arab powers, Donald Trump was able to find convincing discussion angles to encourage the establishment of a dialogue. He made sure to establish excellent diplomatic and commercial relations with each of them beforehand to give life to his diplomatic project for the Middle East. This does not mean that it was an exceptional maneuver, but it did have the merit of calming certain resentments by focusing actors who were traditionally not very close on a common adversary. By doing so, President Biden is calling into question these diplomatic agreements at the risk of provoking new upheavals between Israel and the Arab states of the region. Ultimately, therein lies the problem: what about the diplomatic recognition that Jerusalem made with Abu Dhabi and Riyadh a few months ago?

The Biden Administration is not as favored by Prime Minister Netanyahu as the previous one. However, by blocking any form of intervention by the Security Council, the United States is providing a kind of support for Israel's action. Need we recall, however, that Joe Biden is presiding over a country that voted for him by a majority because of his predecessor's mismanagement of a health crisis? Since then, the financial sector has been fearful of decisions coming from the White House. The same is true for some former senior US military officers who have made public a written letter in which they question the mental health of the 46th President of the United States... and the validity of the presidential election! This reopens old chapters which seemed to be definitively closed in the United States, but which betray above all a social and political malaise which is still perceptible despite the efforts deployed by Joe Biden to try to appease a sensitive social climate.

Certainly, we can give credit to the Democratic President for decisions that have ensured that the American population has been calmed or reassured and that it needed to hear reassuring words and see them followed up. In this sense, the communication and the decisions taken in terms of fighting the spread of Covid-19 and social tensions, which the Trump Administration had failed to take, were unquestionably welcome. His economic stimulus plan is already more contested. As for his foreign policy, it is dangerous. He has probably long since sketched out a course of action that is in line with what was promoted in his time by the Obama Administration, but which was then contradicted by the foreign policy deployed by Donald Trump. However, the first limits were clearly displayed when he made the strategic mistake of publicly announcing his intention to restart the discussion process on the Iranian nuclear issue during the presidential election campaign. In substance, the idea is undoubtedly good, but it is in form that a mistake was made. By announcing such a willingness, he was going to stir up trouble in the Middle East and jeopardize the feeble semblance of "balance" attempted by Donald Trump, because by positioning himself in this way, he was going to attract the distrust of Jerusalem, Abu Dhabi, and Riyadh. On the other hand, it gave Tehran the opportunity to express itself. Rather than showing any recognition or gratitude for the intention of the then Democratic candidate, the Iranian regime immediately saw this as a means of pressure to be exploited: this led to the operation to further enrich uranium to best negotiate its position in future multiparty talks.

Since then, the United States has been adamant about always standing firm, especially regarding Saudi Arabia, which has been forced to cut back on American military involvement or support, and other decisions that have upset the Wahhabi kingdom's highest officials. Joe

Biden clearly does not share the friendship with the Crown Prince that Donald Trump had built up. Saudi Arabia is now obliged to review its position on Iran, against a backdrop of American pressure, but the question is to determine for how long. Indeed, American support for Israel will undoubtedly reshuffle the cards in the Middle East, especially since President Biden does not seem to be unanimously supported in his country. In our view, he has risked opening a Pandora's box in the Middle East.

The image of this famous box is even more well-founded in that there is a deliberate desire not to ease tensions through traditional diplomatic channels, those through which the chances of success or of obtaining a result would be greatest. In this case, for such a complex conflict, the United Nations is the most credible diplomatic option... if the Security Council can reach an agreement... This is precisely what is lacking since the United States has shown no willingness to continue discussions within the UN forum. On the other hand, Secretary of State Antony Blinken has called on Israel and the Palestinian Authority to remain calm, urging them to spare the civilian population, which is effectively the first victim of these clashes. Clearly, to put on a good face, the State Department has shown empathy by calling for appeasement, but the reality shows that this is mainly a communication stunt aimed at ensuring that the United States does not have to assume the bad role of "peace blocker". This communication is indecent insofar as it will not bring about any concrete results. To put it another way, this strategy consists of showing that Washington cares little about the consequences of such a confrontation, especially for the civilian populations on both sides. The United States has no intention of bringing even a glimmer of diplomatic resolution to this umpteenth crisis.

This eternal repetition of a bilateral crisis is dangerous in more ways than one. Prime Minister Netanyahu is using these armed exchanges to dilute or dissolve an internal political crisis that has lasted for too many months, a crisis in which he is unable to build a majority coalition. By engaging in a new confrontation with Palestine, even though the target is Hamas, he seeks to appeal to the hardest right wing of the national political spectrum, the political wing that is intransigent towards the Palestinian neighbor. Thus, there is an element of internal political calculation. Secondly, by positioning itself in this way, the United States is in the process of confirming a disruption of the fragile geopolitical balance that had been struck earlier with the Abraham Accords. The latter sealed diplomatic recognition between Israel and the United Arab Emirates, which in turn heralded a new dialogue between Israel and Saudi Arabia. By confronting Hamas, Israel has thrown a spanner in the works of the Arab world, and recent diplomatic agreements are naturally threatened, but the role played by the United States may force these Arab actors to accept the situation in a positive light.

The problems of the Middle East are as sensitive as ever and seem more threatening than ever, because beyond the direct confrontation between Israel and the Palestinian Authority, a domino effect can be induced at any moment, including the scenario that would see the Arab powers "disassociate" from the diplomatic maneuvers initiated by Donald Trump to form a common front against Iran. Finally, let us remember that American foreign policy has long been clumsy and even ill-intentioned. Should we recall the reasons that led Uncle Sam's country to engage in armed conflict in Iraq in the early 2000s? The official reasons given were spurious. The United States feared that Saudi Arabia would implode from inside, and that the Wahhabi kingdom would no longer be able to meet American oil needs. It was then that the Bush Administration and the neo-conservatives saw Iraq as a solution to the possible loss of oil supplies from Saudi Arabia. Doubt is therefore permitted as to Washington's real intentions. Thus, what is the Biden Administration trying to do? If the intention is to provoke a new geopolitical upheaval, the gamble is not only risky, but it is very likely that the risk will not be controlled. The American position on this new Israeli-Palestinian crisis is not ambiguous. It is perfectly clear, but it goes against a diplomatic resolution of the tensions. The message is thus addressed to the actors who have dealt with the Trump Administration (apart from Israel, which was nevertheless very close to the relational circles of Donald Trump and his son-in-law Jared Kushner). It is also clear that a message has been sent to Moscow and Beijing by destroying the chances of diplomatic success in the Security Council.

As we can see, this umpteenth Israeli-Palestinian opposition implies external interests that are emerging or that simply tend to confirm that the world of the 21st century is multipolar. In the meantime, any new major crisis in the Middle East can lead to the fear of the worst, i.e., the risk of a geographical spread of the crisis zones and possibly the return in force of terrorist organizations that could again disturb international security in the short term. Diplomatic crisis resolution is a complex art, and sometimes diplomatic solutions fail, especially in the Middle East crises. On the other hand, by refusing to resolve the Israeli-Palestinian confrontation under the aegis of the United Nations, the United States may have activated a Leviathan against which it will be even more difficult to fight.

Meanwhile, initiatives are multiplying to start a diplomatic movement. France has submitted a resolution to the United Nations Security Council, while at the regional level, Egypt and Jordan are working to ease tensions. The whole of the Middle East fears the scenario of a conflagration spreading over a wider area. On May 19, for the first time, President Biden called on Israel to quickly "de-escalate". This call is the first sign of annoyance from the White House. It is indeed a sign of annoyance because the risk of an uncontrollable degeneration is real. President Biden's challenge is to ensure that he does not create a new rift with Israel other than the disagreement over Iran, but Prime Minister Netanyahu has imposed himself in force, both on the national and international scene. The United States probably should have reacted earlier and not blocked the discussions in the Security Council. All this is part of a great diplomatic game in which the major players in world diplomacy are testing each other. Moreover, the American blockage before the Security Council comes just a short time before a summit meeting between Joe Biden and Vladimir Putin, which seems to be under discussion. We must therefore perceive in it a desire on the part of the resident of the White House to show his power before meeting his Russian counterpart. We thus understand the stakes at the heart of the concerns, but the American position was undoubtedly motivated mainly by strategic and tactical considerations that do not seem to us to be the most opportune. Finally, it appears that UN diplomacy seems ineffective and that that of the European Union has been shattered by the inconsistency of a collegial approach put forward by the Brussels institutions. Indeed, there are disagreements on the understanding of this crisis within the member states, and France has taken the initiative of submitting a resolution to the Security Council, an institution of which it is also a permanent member.

We cannot end this post without questioning the relevance of the American position which, in our opinion, is very risky for the already very fragile balance in the Middle

East. We are aware of the complexity of the issues at stake. Moreover, they are multiple. These recurring conditions mean that any new crisis can quickly tip over into a situation of lack of control, especially when it involves the State of Israel and the Palestinian Authority. As far as international diplomacy is concerned, we can see that it is paralyzed or parasitic by other interests, notably those defended by the world's greatest political powers, which test each other. Therefore, we ask the question: by not intervening in a collegial process aimed at finding a solution to this crisis, has the United States taken the measure of the risks that could at any moment spill over and generate unfortunate consequences on a larger scale?

The reality is that European diplomacy is not coordinated on this issue, while the limits of UN action have been reached because of the unwillingness of a member state of the Security Council to work collegially on a resolution that would not necessarily have led to an easing of tensions between Israel and the Palestinian Authority. On the other hand, if the United States wants to show its power of influence on the international political scene, this attitude risks cooling or disappointing its traditional allies, the very ones who distanced themselves from Washington during the Trump presidency. The spirit of collegiality and openness to dialogue with the rest of the international community may thus be called into question. The United States is defending a position that is not directly concerned with the risks of escalating tensions between Israel and Palestine. Its real concern is with the reactions that its position may induce in Moscow and Beijing. The real signal was indeed intended for these two important political powers. The problem remains that it is necessary to urgently tackle the task of finding a way out of a crisis that is not contained and whose consequences may drag on and, above all, spread geographically. Time may prove Joe Biden and Antony

Blinken right, but our overall feeling is that of a misjudgment, as Washington is ultimately trying to understand the reactions of Moscow and Beijing to this resurgence of Israeli-Palestinian tensions. It also shows how divided the world is, and how damaging the clash of conflicting interests is to any form of diplomacy as well as to global security. Diplomacy may not be able to solve the Israeli-Palestinian crisis because a diplomatic victory depends on the will and consent of individuals. On the other hand, if diplomacy fails when there was an opportunity to engage in a dialogue that would not necessarily have led to a victorious outcome, then there would be much to regret... and many unanswered questions about the functioning of the United Nations Security Council, which would then become, despite itself, given the spirit in which it was originally created, the council of global insecurity.

***

On the night of May 20-21, 2021, a ceasefire was finally reached and signified the cessation of hostilities between Hamas and the State of Israel. During the ten days or so that the crisis lasted, several hundred deaths were deplored on the Palestinian side and a little more than a dozen on the Israeli side. The human toll was heavy. As for the political consequences, the ceasefire was obtained thanks to an Egyptian intervention supported by pressure from Washington. In the wake of the agreement reached, Secretary of State Antony Blinken announced his intention to travel to the Middle East as soon as possible to meet the main Israeli and Palestinian leaders. The course of events shows once again the failure of UN coordination to find a way out of the crisis. While the New York-based international institution is not to blame, it is the American attitude that is of concern, since the failure of the United Nations to act is the result of American blocking from the very first days of the Israeli-Palestinian crisis. There was a clear desire on the part of Washington to disrupt the game and to thwart UN diplomacy: a message was thus sent to China, Russia and to the European Union, which seems to be less and less united, while since the Brexit, only France now represents the club of the twenty-seven within the permanent UN Security Council. Finally, despite appearances, the Abraham Accords of August 2020 are not in question. Indeed, the Arab countries seem to consider that they have obtained more advantages than disadvantages in their diplomatic relations with Israel since the signing of the agreements.

This is a summary of the situation surrounding the ceasefire: let us not be afraid to say that, although American diplomacy intends to invest rapidly in the Middle East, many questions remain unanswered. Indeed, despite the validity of the Abraham Accords and the end of hostilities between Israel and the Gaza Strip, we cannot help but compare the Middle East to a supermassive volcano on the verge of an extraordinary eruption. This is the immense challenge that awaits Antony Blinken: to make diplomacy triumph where it has largely failed until now, to calm and tranquilize in the long term a region condemned to face multiple, lasting, and humanly dramatic crises. The errors of the past have certainly contributed to the increasing fragility of a region that validated its modern borders at the end of the First World War, but which has only augured permanent disorder, not to mention the political destabilization provoked by foreign powers, which has only aggravated a deleterious ambient climate. We wish we were wrong, but the question is: how long will the truce of hostilities last? Similarly, are we sure that Israel's armed intervention will not eventually be a source of old resentment felt by its Arab diplomatic partners?

Diplomacy and international relations are unfortunately not exact disciplines. Everything can change at great speed and take unexpected directions. Yet, in the case of Middle Eastern tensions, we are fairly convinced that all possible diplomatic efforts will not suffice to bring lasting peace to a region plagued by multiple, long-standing, and terribly persistent annoyances. Hate is very much on the rise compared to love, even though political leaders are advocating peace solutions. It would be wrong to believe that everyone "agrees" on wanting to wage war. People are tired and bruised by so many years of conflict and too short-lived episodes of peace. However, in the light of events, a lasting peace seems illusory if not impossible. Raymond Aron's impossible peace and improbable war during the Cold War could in many ways become possible peace and probable war for the Middle East.

Indeed, if local decisionmakers were able to reach agreement, there is nothing to indicate that differences of interest between the world's major political powers would not challenge efforts initiated by local decisionmakers. The first step would be for them to agree on a principle of lasting peace. As we have just seen, the American position within the United Nations Security Council has above all highlighted a divergence of views on how to approach the Israeli-Palestinian crisis. The result is that this procrastination within the Security Council is the result of a state strategy to assert its diplomatic power to the other "big boys" of this world. The United States is now determined to tackle Israeli-Palestinian relations head-on, to show Russia and China that it remains the dominant diplomatic power in Middle East issues. It is now up to Antony Blinken to find the right words to calm a potentially explosive context and to be able to affirm that the Biden Administration has implemented effective diplomacy in a region where American diplomacy has often wanted to show itself as dominant but where it has mostly brought about disorder. Although he has often been challenged for his highly atypical diplomatic vision, Donald Trump has succeeded where his predecessors have failed in the past: to establish a dialogue and seal an agreement between states traditionally not very friendly towards each other.

Victory of the ultraconservative Raissi in Iran
June 2021

It was a ballot eagerly awaited by the international community: the Iranian presidential election, the first round of which was held on June 18, 2021. Although the election is normally held over two rounds, the ultraconservative Ebrahim Raissi obtained nearly 62% of the votes cast in the first round, thus winning the election, and succeeding Hassan Rouhani, who could not run for a third presidential term. The main highlight was the high abstention rate, which once again confirms the prevailing unease in Iran between the admittedly numerous supporters of the clerics and ultraconservatives, while the others hope for a change in governance and the end of the era of the heirs of the 1979 Islamic Revolution. The unease is all the greater because the country is suffering from severe economic sanctions aimed at stifling the regime, which nevertheless manages to maintain an unchanging course of political governance. Many Iranians have left their country to live in other countries, hoping for a better life experience elsewhere. For those who cannot leave their country, they protest by refusing to vote. Ebrahim Raissi won the presidential election by a wide margin, just days after the G7 meetings, the NATO summit in Brussels and the first meeting between Presidents Biden and Putin. This election also comes in a tense global geopolitical context, especially in the Middle East where tensions are higher than ever. While waiting to understand what the new Iranian President intends to do in terms of diplomacy, first impressions suggest that President Biden's desire to renew dialogue with Iran will come up against a major problem: Ebrahim Raissi arouses many fears among his regional rivals, a context that may tempt him to maintain a hostile discourse towards them. This would complicate American diplomatic wishes and play into the hands of China and Russia. As for the nuclear issue, there is nothing to indicate that the regime's new strongman is inclined to revive a dialogue that was brutally broken off by Donald Trump while the other parties tried to find common ground with Tehran.

Although more than one in two voters refused to go to the polls, Ebrahim Raissi won the election. The abstention rate was indeed 51.2%, a record since the establishment of the Islamic Revolution. The reactions in the world are very revealing of the state of diplomacy towards Iran: the result of the election has only confirmed the sympathies or alliances of some states while others naturally castigate the victory of the ultraconservatives. Two countries have not hidden their satisfaction: Turkey and Syria. Ankara and Damascus have indeed commented in very friendly terms on the victory of Ebrahim Raissi. For President Erdogan, this victory is *"beneficial for the Iranian people"*, a way of showing his appreciation after having been discreet at the NATO summit in Brussels a few days earlier. By communicating in this way, he is showing the other members of NATO that he intends to pursue the diplomacy he wants, without worrying about external opinions. As for Bashar al-Assad, he sent his warm congratulations to the winner, saying that the election result was undoubtedly excellent news for the continuation of the fight against external pressure. President Putin's reaction was more subtle but clearly a message to his Western rivals: *"relations between our countries are traditionally friendly and good neighborly. I hope that your activities in this high post will contribute to the further development of constructive bilateral cooperation in various fields, as well as our partnership in international affairs."* [14]

---

[14] *"Les principales réactions internationales à l'élection de Ebrahim Raïssi en Iran"*, www.ouest-france.fr, June 19, 2021 Translation done by the author from French quote.

As for the State of Israel, the result of the election is clearly castigated. It was quickly denounced as electoral manipulation that probably does not reflect the reality of the situation according to Jerusalem. It was indeed expected that Israel would not look kindly on an ultraconservative victory that will undoubtedly perpetuate complicated diplomatic relations between the two countries. Finally, the reaction of the son of the last Shah of Iran was puzzling when he declared on social networks that the Iranian people showed *"unity and solidarity"* by *"boycotting and saying no to the authoritarian Iranian regime."* [15] This is undoubtedly a matter of interpretation and appreciation, but short of interpreting the high abstention rate as a concrete action against the country's rulers, we interpret it more as an expressed weariness and disinterest that was clearly expressed by a part of the electorate. Overall, few international actors have welcomed Ebrahim Raissi's victory. This augurs well for years to come, during which Iran will undoubtedly continue its delicate diplomacy with the Western world. That is the overall impression. As for the Iranian people, we feel above all a form of frustration among those who did not wish to express their voice at the ballot box.

---

[15] *Ibid.* Translation done by the author from French quote.

Tensions, uncertainties and Covid
May 2021

The end of the first half of 2021 is a continuation of what the 2020 vintage was: a great global mess that keeps growing. As far as the health crisis is concerned, there seems to be some improvement since several vaccines flooded the world market. While we thought we were finally getting the upper hand on this disease that has been striking the planet for a year and a half, new variants are appearing, and the medical profession is seriously questioning the effectiveness of the vaccines marketed against these new forms of Covid. The Indian variant is frightening because of the damage observed in patients. It seems to be more contagious and aggressive. The fear is of course that it will spread rapidly on a global scale and that it will cause further major health and economic disruptions. This would be one more annoyance when there are already so many others! The end of the Israeli-Palestinian hostilities is based on a precarious balance. Any new event is likely to set off a new fire.

In the United States, President Biden is going on the offensive with a request for a report from the intelligence services to determine the true origin of the Covid-19, a maneuver designed to put pressure on China but which, on closer inspection, looks like a "one stone, two shots" operation. Indeed, the idea is also to expose the Trump Administration to possible past turpitude... What did it really know? Did it intentionally hide information? It is therefore to be expected that the results provided by the intelligence agencies will be the cause of the outbreak of hostilities against China or the Trump clan, or both at the same time. It is not impossible to imagine that the results provided by the intelligence services point to a truth largely hidden by Beijing and that the true origin of the Covid comes from a laboratory; on the other hand, that President Trump, in his time, would have had wind of information that he would not have communicated or that he would have voluntarily spread fake news on the subject with the sole aim of reversing the course of an electoral campaign that was then unfavorable to him.

As for the many uncertainties, it is difficult to draw up an exhaustive list of what we could call "anomalies to global welfare". For example, we can cite the case of Iran holding some Westerners captive on suspicion of espionage. This may be the case. Or it may not be the case and it may be a political strategy to put pressure on the international community in response to the strict economic sanctions that Tehran is under and hopes to see eased in future negotiations on the nuclear issue. Meanwhile, Iran's strategy is to apply pressure to make its voice better heard and to show a firmness that indicates a desire not to sit down with the other parties to the dialogue in the position of an expiatory victim. Iran intends to put forward its arguments and not give in to any external pressure. The message has already been sent to Washington... When we talk about Iran, we can't help but talk about oil. Let's remember that terrible financial crisis suffered by the oil sector in March and April 2020 as the Covid-19 pandemic began to spread around the world. Since then, trading prices have recovered and have been fluctuating between $60 and $70 per barrel of Brent for several months. However, this level of trading price is not satisfactory for most of the world's major producers who would like to be able to sell at a higher price. The problem is that the OPEC cartel would also like to be able to initiate a new phase of upwardly oriented production. This desire is understandable, but now a shadow is hanging over the global oil market: the Indian variant!

Meanwhile, we are also witnessing a great cacophony on the international financial markets. During the health crisis, the most powerful high-tech companies recorded record balance sheets and their major shareholders saw their personal fortunes jump. Yet, although the ten-year trend in US Treasury bonds does not seem to herald a financial crisis in the making, the global atmosphere generated by Covid has, all in all, derailed something: a certain madness has taken hold of the world with a frenzied hyper-speculation that has taken hold of many individuals who act with the financial markets as if the discovery of gold in a river will trigger a new rush. We are thinking for example of cryptocurrencies which, for some of them, have the wind in their sails and see many individuals trying their luck by betting a few savings in the hope of seeing them sur-multiply in record time. For the blow, some were able to make good deals and will not complain to have invested at the right time. They benefit from an unhoped-for windfall or reap the benefits of a carefully planned strategy. Others have lost a lot by investing at the top, betting on a continued rise in exchange prices when prices have suddenly fallen. However, the evolution of cryptocurrency prices does not follow a simple logic of supply and demand. We realize that it doesn't take much to influence exchange prices up or down. The big boss of Tesla acted as a guru for Bitcoin when he decided to invest heavily in this value and to offer Tesla customers to pay for their car purchases in this cryptocurrency... The effect was dazzling, and Bitcoin reached a record value. A few days later, the opposite effect occurred when the same Elon Musk declared that he no longer wanted to offer payments in Bitcoin, citing a surprising reason: this cryptocurrency pollutes too much! It is understood that Elon Musk knows perfectly well how Bitcoins are generated... Yet, his words are so valuable that with just a few words he can send the financial markets into a tizzy. He is part of a very closed circle of individuals with this power.

For the average person, this period is nebulous. It is difficult to understand what is going on around us and to accept decisions that do not seem to be coherent or that involve restrictions on freedom. Let's take the example of this idea of a vaccine passport. We understand the desire of states to allow their citizens to move around more freely, to return to a normal life, and for the economy to return to normal activity. However, the idea of this passport is not well perceived because in the eyes of many people, it is a barely disguised way of forcing everyone to go and get vaccinated, despite all the controversies that have arisen around the production of vaccines in record time. Very explicitly, many people do not trust the political authorities because they did not communicate well at the height of the health crisis. There was an incessant telescoping of contradictory information that gave a double impression: first, it tended to make people believe that the governing authorities were overwhelmed, clueless or even incompetent in the face of the reality of the situation. Secondly, that state lies had been carefully disseminated to the greatest number of people to hide information that had to be kept secret. All these uncertainties and contradictions contributed to feed popular fantasies which above all marked a growing misunderstanding between decisionmakers and citizens. Many of the citizens have reached a point of frustration because of all the prejudices they have suffered: loss of jobs, loss of income, changes in working conditions with the increased promotion of teleworking, social ties at half-mast, and a whole host of psychological states that have deteriorated because of this painful life experience for many of them, who hope to finally see the end of the tunnel. Covid has not only caused deaths. It has caused a lot of collateral damage. The longer the health crisis lasts, the greater the chances of a widening of the gap between the ruling elites and the citizens, who will put up with less and less with decisions for which they will denounce misunderstandings or even inconsistencies, whether they are founded or not. The risk is to generate an automatic effect where any new decision will be criticized.

In Europe, national elections will soon be held in Germany in 2021 and in France in 2022. They may offer a new political landscape for Berlin and Paris, but also for the European Union (EU), which has relied heavily on the French-German relationship as the locomotive in the twenty-seven-club since the United Kingdom effectively withdrew after tumultuous negotiations following the Brexit referendum. The Brexit has probably not yet delivered all its unfortunate consequences. We are thinking of the desire expressed by the Scottish leadership to rejoin the EU. This is just one of many thorny issues. In another area, when we talk about the United Kingdom and the EU, how can we not mention the strained diplomatic relations with Russia or Turkey? Considering these two countries, Western opinion is different.

As far as Ankara is concerned, many questions remain concerning the true intentions of President Erdogan, who knows how to stir up the Western world for different reasons. If he plays with fire, he also knows how to thwart the plans of the EU and those of NATO. He is also able to play on the ultra-fluctuating relations with Russia. With his alter ego Vladimir Putin, they have a tumultuous relationship that is hardly surprising given the strategies deployed by both.

On the other hand, as far as Russia's relations with the Western world are concerned, the situation is particular insofar as it is designated as the easy enemy. It is easy to impute many evils to Russia, sometimes well-founded and sometimes more dubious, to maintain complicated relations with Moscow where no one would dare to do so with China. That Russia and the Western world have a complicated relationship is undeniable. That Russia has launched cyberattack campaigns, that seems to be the case. However, in all these criticisms of Russia, there is a reciprocity. It is almost amusing to see how the United States takes pains to present Russia as a threat to the world when the real American rival is surely China, a country with which Russia has a relationship of mutual distrust. When we compare the American and Russian defense budgets, the multiplier coefficient is almost ten in favor of the United States. The Chinese defense budget is three times higher than that of Russia. One should not underestimate Russian intentions, but it would undoubtedly be a good idea to calm down somewhat the maintenance of diplomatic relations that are constantly reminiscent of the Cold War. In the eyes of the United States, China certainly represents a threat of a different level than that represented by Russia. Moscow is not able to challenge American leadership in global hard and soft power in the way that Beijing can now do. We must ask ourselves the right questions. Does what we have just described belong to the world of chance? Probably not. There is a link, a logic that belongs to a very small cenacle of individuals who reign unchallenged over the others, who ally themselves or confront each other, leaving the greatest number of people as spectators of a global context that has never seemed so tense for a long time.

New Covid-19 variant, new concerns
November 2021

Almost two years after the appearance or rather the media coverage of the Covid-19 pandemic, the first lesson is that despite the vaccination campaigns conducted on all continents, this form of coronavirus continues to strike on a large scale and to claim victims. Secondly, its survival also disturbs many people, since some states are closing their borders again or are deciding on internal measures that are sure to fuel controversy and raise questions about fundamental rights. Thus, the Austrian government wanted to move towards a policy of temporary confinement of non-vaccinated individuals. This desire was quickly abandoned in view of the following question: can one demand that a non-vaccinated individual stay at home? In short, the Covid affair continues to poison the existence of the public authorities, who once again find themselves forced to make decisions that will not satisfy everyone. France has opted for a more subtle solution: reducing the validity period of antigenic or PCR tests. Beyond the medical and sanitary aspects, the so-called Omicron variant is about to cause a new wave of concern. In the field of mass distribution, it is whispered that the price of many products will soon increase due to supply problems that will increase transportation costs. Similarly, oil trading prices, which ironically were at their highest during COP 26 in Glasgow for more than three years, are beginning to be impacted by fears about the Omicron variant. By the end of November 2021, in just a few days, Brent crude oil trading prices had fallen by more than 10%.

The appearance of the Omicron variant is obviously not good news. From a health point of view, it is unfortunately to be expected that it will continue to be rampant and to claim victims. As for the world economy, it will undoubtedly suffer the consequences of a slowdown in the economic dynamism that is taking shape. In addition to the economic difficulties, this uncomfortable period is most likely to bring out international tensions. When economic conditions become more complicated, this is usually the time when rivalries are exacerbated. The context is heavy. The great unknown remains the age-old question: how long will this pandemic continue to trouble the world? In this reflection, it is certain that we will not provide an answer to this question. Instead, the idea is to try to determine what the consequences of a new pandemic episode that raises so many fears might be. Indeed, the longer this health crisis lasts, the greater the economic consequences are likely to be. We keep in mind this unfortunate episode of March and April 2020 when, after an unsuccessful consultation within the OPEC + alliance, oil exchange prices had literally plummeted to this unheard-of situation, a few weeks later, when they were at a negative level. In other words, stockholders theoretically had to pay buyers to offload their oil, witnessing this glaring imbalance in which supply far outstripped global demand. It is too premature to imagine such a scenario in a repeat version. Similarly, it is likely that the circumstances that led to such an extreme context will not recur. That said, the longer the pandemic crisis continues, the more negative fluctuations the financial markets will be exposed to.

A new leap into the unknown

Its name is Omicron. This is the name by which the new variant is now known and is terrorizing the world. It worries many. While we are in the middle of a vaccination campaign, a question arises: will the vaccines be effective against this new variant? Public authorities are wondering. What should be done? In some jurisdictions, it has already been decided to re-confine part of the population, to restrict freedom of movement to avoid a rapid spread of the virus and to limit the risks of new tragedies. Telecommuting is back on the agenda. The validity of health passes is being reduced to raise awareness of vaccination. In addition, certain events are making the headlines, such as the Portuguese championship soccer match where a team took the field with only nine able-bodied players, giving rise to numerous negative reactions and criticisms regarding the non-reporting of the match. It turns out that many of the Belenenses players had been affected by the Omicron variant. Beyond the health questions, a doubt remains: how to manage economically this new wave that will undoubtedly fall on the world?

Many states have already taken on large debts to deal with the previous waves. Their economic health has suffered. Likewise, many companies are worried and fear a definitive cessation of their activity. As for the financial markets, after having been crowned by historic performances, the state of grace seems to be fading. The oil markets are tumbling at high speed. At the beginning of December, the price of Brent crude oil has just had some worrying days. On 30 November, the barrel of Brent was traded at $71 compared to $85 a few days earlier, notably during the COP 26 in Glasgow when it had reached a peak not seen since before the Covid-19 crisis. The Omicron variant is sweeping the planet and an impression of déjà vu is taking shape: are we going to see a further sharp decline in global demand for raw materials?

The need for good institutional communication
This scenario is credible given that in Western Europe, many consumer goods have seen their prices rise significantly. In France, the price of electricity has risen by more than 20%. The price increase also applies to gasoline and many foodstuffs. This variation in prices is explained by the supply difficulties encountered by transporters. Some

countries are worried about a possible shortage of certain consumer goods. In other words, there is concern in a global context of short-term uncertainty. In France, public decisionmakers are more worried about this bad news as 2022 will be an election year. An accumulation of bad news in the run-up to the end of the year is obviously not a good thing for these public decisionmakers. However, they must take their responsibilities and decide. This is precisely what is being done by the French government in view of the appearance of the Omicron variant. The most difficult part remains institutional communication: getting people to accept decisions for the good of the general interest. This is a difficult task insofar as France, like many other countries, has been suffering for nearly two years from this health crisis, and many people do not see any short-term solution. This is where the problem lies: how much longer will all this go on? Institutional communication is therefore essential to facilitate the acceptance of decisions by the greatest number.

It is difficult to give good advice to policy makers because we have all been dealing with this health crisis for too long. For the public, the prevailing feeling is one of weariness. When will all this end? When will we be able to return to normal life? Does anyone have a clear and well-founded idea? The public authorities have no other option than to recognize that we must learn to live with this regularly mutating form of coronavirus. The problem is that they have no assurance in managing the health crisis. The public authorities seem indeed helpless in front of the resistance of the Covid despite the intense world campaign of vaccination. Moreover, the longer the health crisis lasts, the more negative public opinion will be towards the public decisionmakers. It will oscillate between incompetence and suspicion of lying or withholding information. In other words, it is the bond of trust between elected politicians and their constituents that is likely to suffer from a long prolongation of the health crisis. Citizens are tired of the "vaccination versus anti-vaccination" debate, in which public authorities endorse decisions that are not well accepted. When public authorities denounce the attitude of individuals who refuse vaccination, most people ask that they communicate more clearly and transparently about the reality of Covid-19. Until proven otherwise, in democratic systems, the elected political actor is normally accountable to the electorate that has placed its trust in him. Let the decisionmakers simply have the integrity to recognize their current powerlessness rather than opting for a communication that hammers out the same messages repeatedly, which no longer convince the majority.

GLOSSARY OF ABBREVIATIONS

AFP: Agence France-Presse (French international news agency)
AQIM: Al-Qaeda in the Islamic Maghreb
CIA: Central Intelligence Agency
CO2: Carbon dioxide
DoJ: Department of Justice
ECOWAS: Economic Community of West African States
ESG: Environment, Social and Governance
EU: European Union
FBI: Federal Bureau of Investigation
GAFA: Google Amazon Facebook Apple
GAFAM: Google Amazon Facebook Apple Microsoft
GHG: Greenhouse gases
IEA: International Energy Agency
INSEE: National Institute of Statistics and Economic Studies (French institute of statistics)
IPCC: Intergovernmental Panel on Climate Change
KYC: Know Your Client
LNG: Liquefied Natural Gas
LPG: Liquefied Petroleum Gas
NATO: North Atlantic Treaty Organization
NFT: Non-Fungible Tokens
NPT: Non-Proliferation Treaty
NRA: National Rifle Association
OBOR: One Belt, One Road
OPEC: Organization of the Petroleum Exporting Countries
PDVSA: Petróleos de Venezuela, SA
SCO: Shanghai Cooperation Organization
SME: Small and Medium Enterprises
TOE: Tons of Oil Equivalent
UN: United Nations
USSR: Union of Soviet Socialist Republics
WHO: World Health Organization
WTI: West Texas Intermediate
WTO: World Trade Organization